Visual QuickStart Guide

FileMaker Pro 3

for Macintosh

C. Ann Brown

Peachpit Press

Visual QuickStart Guide
FileMaker Pro 3 for Macintosh
C. Ann Brown

Peachpit Press

2414 Sixth Street
Berkeley, CA 94710
(800) 283-9444
(510) 548-4393
(510) 548-5991 (fax)

Find us on the World Wide Web at: http://www.peachpit.com.

Peachpit Press is a division of Addison Wesley Longman.

© 1996 by C. Ann Brown

Editorial assistance, John Hammett

Production, C. Ann Brown

Notice of Rights

Notice of Liability

ISBN: 0-201-88357-0

0 9 8 7 6 5 4 3 2 1

Printed and bound in the United States of America

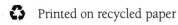 Printed on recycled paper

Contents

Chapter 4 **Working with fields**

Chapter 5 **Formatting text & fields**

Contents

Chapter 12 **Importing & recovering data**

Chapter 13 **Mail merge**

Chapter 14 **Printing & Help**

Chapter 15 **Modems & networks**

Appendix A **Functional Formulas**

Appendix B **Installing FileMaker Pro 3**

This book is dedicated to my aunts, Lucille Smalley and Tommye Gene Welch, and my dear friend J'ann Tolman—without their assistance and their faith in me none of this would have been possible.

Also, sincere thanks to Richard Cohn for putting up with me throughout all of this.

Special thanks to John Hammett for being a fine guiding hand throughout the project.

FileMaker Pro 3 concepts

■ What is a database?

A database is a collection of related information divided into fields and records. Database application programs are used to maintain small or large lists of information, such as mailing lists, library catalogs, and inventory lists, and to create accounting programs.

This chapter acquaints you with how Claris' FileMaker Pro 3 works, shows how to set up a simple database, and introduces some of the terms you need to know before you begin to explore the full power of FileMaker Pro 3.

Before you begin

When you use FileMaker Pro 3, you must create a place for your information to be entered called a *data entry form*.

In order to do this, you start by determining several aspects of the database, including:

▲ Types of information your database will include, such as addresses, names, quantity information, dates, or times

▲ How the screen will look when the data is entered, such as the order in which the fields appear on the screen

▲ How printouts will look, whether they will look different from the data entry form, or whether they will be the same

The data goes in here...

as individual pieces of information—names, addresses, inventory items, prices—anything you want to keep track of.

and comes out there...

organized as output for mailing labels, envelopes, invoices, telephone books, or inventory forms.

■ What is a field or record?

Fields

Think of all of those forms you fill in from day to day, such as car registrations, contest entry blanks, or subscription forms. Typically, each of these forms has a specific place for you to enter information such as your name and address.

Individual areas within a form are called *fields* in a database. The area where you record a name is a field, and the area where you record a street address is yet another field.

Welcome to Qualx Chiropractic
Please fill out our registration card

First name _____ Last name _____
Company _____
Address _____
City _____ State ____ Zip code _____

Telephone number _____
Fax number _____
For emergency contact:

The first and last name positions on this registration card become fields in the database.

First name	Phyllis
Last name	Johnson
Company	ReMarx Realty
Address	792 Stow Ave.
City	Oakland
State	CA
Zip code	94606
Telephone number	510-798-9898
Fax number	9896
First name	Sam
Last name	Long
Company	Jordan Bright
Address	1 Market Plaza
City	San Francisco
State	CA
Zip code	94110
Telephone number	415 322-2232
Fax number	2233

The entire form is one record. All of the records make up the database.

Records

The collection of information filled out on one of these forms is called a *record*. Databases consist of many records, each record containing exactly the same fields.

If a record is a collection of fields, a *database* is a collection of records.

■ Type of information

In FileMaker Pro 3 fields can contain several types of information including:

▲ Text, such as names, addresses, and numbers not used in calculations, such as telephone and fax numbers

▲ Numeric information, such as prices or quantities

▲ Dates or times

▲ Container information, which is information that automatically fills a field as a record is created, such as a serial number

▲ Mathematical calculations, such as finding total price by multiplying number of items sold by the unit price

▲ Summary information for creating subtotals and totals

▲ Global information, for creating temporary information to be used by every record in the database, such as a universal code for that day

Examples of information

Text information	
Social Security numbers	111-11-1111
Telephone numbers	333-4444
Names, addresses	Peachpit Press

Numeric information	
Prices	$39.95
Amounts	14,982
Measurements	4 (feet)

Date or time information	
Birthdays	5/24/45
Data entry time	3:41 PM

Calculation information	
Price times Amount	$39.95 x 14,982

■ Typical database functions

Data entry

It's obvious you enter data in a database, but what might not be so obvious is that you can have FileMaker Pro 3 do some of the entry automatically without your help. Databases can be automated to enter simple items such as:

▲ Today's date or the current time
▲ The operator doing the data entry
▲ Other unique information

You can also enter information by typing or by using cut and paste to transfer information among fields, records, or databases.

Nancy's Automobile Tracking Service

Customer: Carl Spike
Car/Model: Ford Taurus
City: New York, NY

Customer: Rick Banker
Model: Nissan Sentra
City: Sedona, AZ

Search

Search lets you look for:

▲ Specific facts, such as the name of a city
▲ Ranges of information, such as amounts between $5.00 and $10.00
▲ Multiple details, such as everyone who lives in Arizona and who owns a Nissan Sentra but does not own any other type of automobile

Arrange data in City order

Albuquerque, NM
Boston, MA
Canton, OH
Priddy, TX
Washington, DC

Sort

Sort arranges information in the database in any order you wish. You use sort to:

▲ Place a mailing list in state order, then within the state, by zip code order
▲ Arrange accounts payable in date order
▲ Categorize a picture catalog by stock number

Mia's Special Dog Treats

Price $45.00
Quantity   7
Extension $315.00

Calculations

Fields can have information someone enters, or they can contain simple or complex calculations such as:

▲ Multiplying the quantity times the price
▲ Adding a late fee if an account is more than 30 days overdue

Typical database functions

■ What are layouts?

Simply creating a field does not make a database. You need to design a screen that places the fields in position, ready for data entry. This is called creating a *layout*.

Layouts can be used just for data entry on screen, for printing, or for both data entry and printing. Most databases have more than one layout.

The FileMaker Pro 3 menus appear across the top of the layout screen, some tools are provided on the left and bottom of the screen, and the data entry form appears in the center.

The data entry form fields and field labels

FileMaker Pro 3 menus

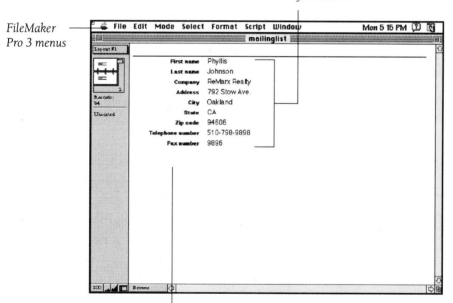

This layout is for entering customer information, including telephone or fax numbers, contact names, and other customer details. Additional layouts could include information for printing labels or invoice forms.

The FileMaker Pro 3 icon starts up the program. You may also double-click an existing database to open it and start FileMaker Pro 3.

If you choose Create a new empty file from the New Database dialog box, then click OK, the New File dialog box appears.

As you create each new field, its name appears in the Define Fields list under Field Name with the type of field listed in the Type column.

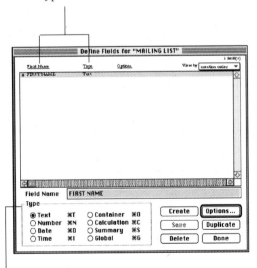

Field types are selected by choosing the proper Type radio button in the Type panel.

■ Getting started

This example starts you with a simple mailing list database and shows you how to begin creating a new database.

Creating a simple mailing list

1. Open FileMaker Pro 3 by double-clicking the FileMaker Pro 3 icon.

2. Choose *Create a new empty file* from the New Database dialog box, then click the OK button. The New File dialog box appears.

3. In the Create a new file named box, type the name `Mailing List` and click the Save button. The Define Fields dialog box appears.

4. In the Type panel, select the Text radio button if it is not already selected.

5. In the Field Name box, type `First name` for the name of the first field and click the Create button.

The First name field appears in the Field Name list at the top of the Define Fields dialog box.

6. Repeat steps 3 through 5 and use the Field Name box to create the following text fields:

▲ Last name   ▲ State
▲ Company   ▲ Zip code
▲ Address   ▲ Telephone number
▲ City   ▲ Fax number

7. Click the Done button when you are finished.

The automatic layout created by FileMaker Pro 3 now appears. Each field, or data entry area, appears with a field label to the right of it. The field labels tell you the name of the field so you can tell where to enter the proper information.

■ Main FileMaker Pro 3 screen

The first FileMaker Pro 3 screen you see shows the automatic layout that is created by FileMaker Pro 3 once you have finished defining your fields.

Entering data

1. In the Browse mode, click to the right of the first field's label. The outline of the field appears.
2. Type the first name of the first person you want to appear in your database.
3. Tap the Tab key to move to the next field and continue filling in the information.
4. When the entire record is full, to obtain a new blank record, choose *New Record* from the Mode menu, or press ⌘-**N** (Command-N).

Record numbers

Records are numbered in the order they are input, with the first record number 1, and each subsequent record number increasing by 1.

If you sort the database, your records will be renumbered beginning with 1. The Rolodex helps you find records by record number.

Click here to begin entering data.

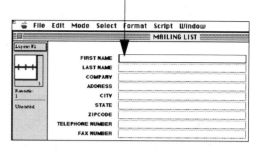

Here is the mailing list database. Notice the fields, which are outlined in light gray dots, and the field labels, which tell you what the names of the fields are.

✔ **Tip:** *To use key combinations such as* ⌘-**N***, first hold down the Command key, tap the letter* **N***, and then let go of the Command key.*

FileMaker Pro 3 menus in the Browse mode

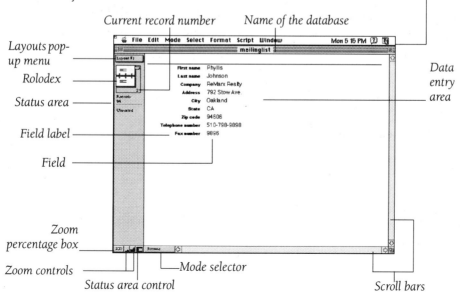

Current record number   *Name of the database*

Layouts pop-up menu

Rolodex

Status area

Field label

Field

Data entry area

Zoom percentage box

Zoom controls

Status area control

Mode selector

Scroll bars

Main FileMaker Pro 3 screen

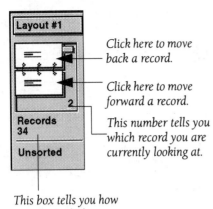

Click here to move back a record.

Click here to move forward a record.

This number tells you which record you are currently looking at.

This box tells you how many records there are in the database.

The location pop-up menu is at the top of the Open File dialog box.

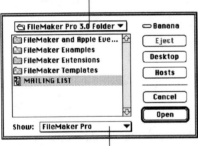

The Show box is set to see FileMaker Pro files as a default. This box also contains options for other types of files.

Keyboard shortcuts

File menu shortcuts	
New file	No shortcut key
Open an existing file	⌘-o
Close a file	⌘-w
Quit FileMaker Pro 3	⌘-Q

Moving around

▲ Click on the bottom page of the Rolodex to move forward a record, or the top page of the Rolodex to move backward a record;
or
▲ Click in the status area and type the record number of the record you wish to move to.

Opening an existing file

1. Choose *Open* from the File menu, or press ⌘-o. The Open File dialog box appears.
2. From the pop-up menu at the top of the Open File dialog box, select the location of your existing file.
3. When the file name appears in the scrolling list, click the file name once to select it then click the Open button, or double-click the file name.

Closing an open file

▲ Choose *Close* from the File menu, or press ⌘-w.

You don't have to save your work. FileMaker Pro 3 takes care of saving your files for you automatically as you enter records.

■ FileMaker modes

Even though you have a simple layout appearing on the screen, there are several ways of looking at this layout.

These first four choices, Browse, Find, Layout, and Preview, are in the Mode menu.

Browse

Browse shows the fields as they appear in normal data entry order. You do not see how many records print on a page or where the page margins are.

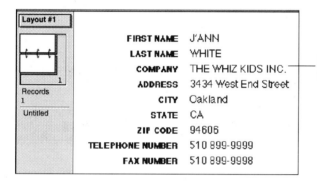

In the Browse mode, you can see data that is entered in the fields.

Find

Find shows the layout in the Find mode, which is used to select information. The fields appear empty, and you type in the information you are looking for in this mode.

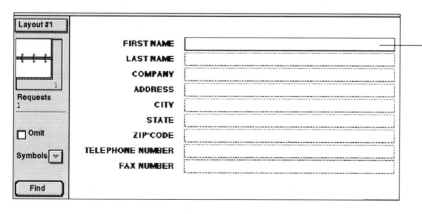

In the Find mode, the fields are empty and you enter information you are looking for in the proper field.

FileMaker modes

Layout

Layout shows the fields without information and is the mode where you rearrange the position of the fields, add text or art, and change formatting such as text formats and field formats.

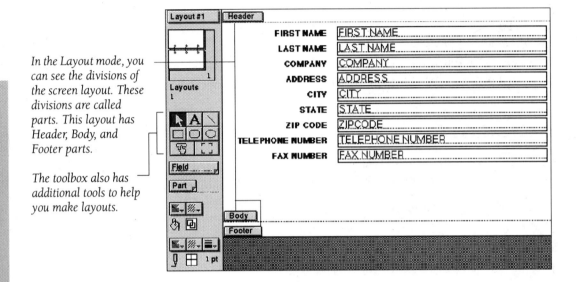

In the Layout mode, you can see the divisions of the screen layout. These divisions are called parts. This layout has Header, Body, and Footer parts.

The toolbox also has additional tools to help you make layouts.

Preview

Preview shows the layout the way it appears when it is printed. You see the page margins in this view and also see how many records print on a page.

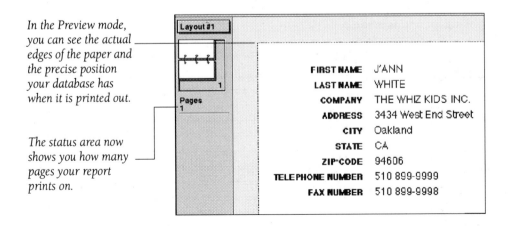

In the Preview mode, you can see the actual edges of the paper and the precise position your database has when it is printed out.

The status area now shows you how many pages your report prints on.

FileMaker modes

To change a FileMaker Pro 3 mode

▲ Choose the mode you wish to use from the Mode menu;

or

▲ Choose the mode selector pop-up menu at the bottom of the screen, and select the mode you wish.

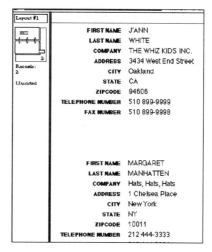

The Mode menu contains commands for changing the view.

Multiple records

View as Form and View as List change how many records you can see on the screen. These two commands are found in the Select menu. They work only with the Browse mode.

View as Form

If you choose View as Form while you are in the Browse mode, you see only one record at a time.

View as List

If you choose View as List while you are in the Browse mode, you see as many records as fit on the screen at one time.

When you choose View as List, you see as many records as possible on your screen. You must be in the Browse mode for this to work.

Selecting a view

1. Choose *Browse* from the Mode menu or from the mode selector pop-up menu.

2. Choose *View as Form* from the Select menu to see one record at a time when you are doing data entry;

or

Choose *View as List* from the Select menu to see more than one record at a time when you are doing data entry.

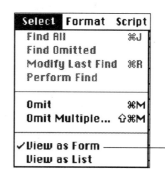

View as Form is chosen here. When you select a view, a check mark appears beside that view.

FileMaker modes

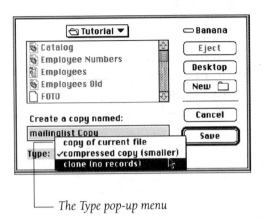

The Type pop-up menu

✔ **Tip:** *To make a quick, efficient backup of your database, choose compressed copy (smaller) from the Type pop-up menu.*

■ Saving a file

As you finish entering a record, that record is automatically saved. For that reason, you find no command to save a file in FileMaker Pro 3.

Saving copies with data

You can save a copy of any database with all of the information in it. This is one way of creating a backup of a file.

To save a copy of a database, including the data:

1. Choose *Save a Copy As* from the File menu. The Create a Copy dialog box appears.
2. Choose the proper location for the copy from the pop-up menu at the top of the Create a Copy dialog box.
3. Type a name in the Create a copy named box.
4. Choose copy of current file in the Type pop-up menu.
5. Click the Save button.

Type pop-up menu

The Type pop-up menu contains three choices:
  ▲ Copy of current file, which saves an exact copy of the file with all of the records in it
  ▲ Compressed copy (smaller), which saves a copy of the file that is smaller in size but contains all of the information
  ▲ Clone (no records), which saves a copy of the file without any information in the file, just the fields, layouts, and automation

Saving empty copies or clones

You can use the clone (no records) choice from the Type pop-up menu when you want to use the same layout as another database.

To save an empty copy of a database:

1. Follow steps 1 through 3 in "Saving copies with data" (above).
2. Choose clone (no records) from the Type pop-up menu.
3. Click the Save button.

■ Document preferences

Document preferences change the way an individual database behaves regarding:

▲ Drag-and-drop text selection
▲ User name
▲ Passwords
▲ Startup layout
▲ How often a file is saved
▲ Modem setup strings, location, and speed
▲ Dialing preferences and locations
▲ Other options

To use document preferences

1. Choose *Preferences* from the Edit menu. The Preferences dialog box appears.
2. Choose the category of preference you wish to change from the Preferences pop-up menu at the top of the Preferences dialog box.
3. Click in the checkboxes or click the radio button for the preferences you wish to activate.
4. Click the Done button.

Edit	Mode	Select
Can't Undo		⌘Z
Cut		⌘X
Copy		⌘C
Paste		⌘U
Clear		
Duplicate		⌘D
Select All		⌘A
Paste Special		▶
Spelling		▶
Preferences...		

Use the Preferences command in the Edit menu to change such items as user name, startup layout, and how often a file is saved.

Preferences

✓General
Document
Layout
Memory
Modem
Dialing

...drop text selection
...New dialog

○ System "Anna Marie"
● Custom

Network protocol: <none> ▼

Done

■ What's new in FileMaker Pro 3

FileMaker Pro 3 still looks very much like FileMaker Pro 2, and it features the same ease-of-use and intuitive menu design that makes FileMaker so easy to understand. This new release includes features that enhance the performance of FileMaker and dramatically increase the capabilities of this outstanding database program.

New features

Feature	Explanation	See pages
Automatic database creation	Have a file in another database or format? Just import it into FileMaker Pro 3 and the program does all of the hard work for you.	See Chapter 12, "Importing & recovering data" on page 161.
Relational database performance	You can "borrow" data from another database and keep your file sizes small and your work-load lighter.	See Chapter 11, "Relational concepts" on page 149.
Automatic mail merge	Do your mail merge right from FileMaker Pro 3.	See Chapter 13, "Mail merge" on page 171.
Modem capability	You can fax or modem layouts and data directly from FileMaker Pro 3.	See Chapter 15, "Modems & networks" on page 189.
Increased file size	This new version lets you have 50 separate databases open at the same time, and each database can be ten times larger than FileMaker Pro 2 files.	See FileMaker Pro 3 reference manual
Cross-platform compatibility	You can share files with many other computing platforms without having to translate files and information for that specific platform.	See FileMaker Pro 3 reference manual

Data access & editing

■ Access privileges

You can limit access to your FileMaker Pro 3 files by setting the access privileges and choosing a password for other users or groups of users. To limit access to FileMaker Pro 3 data to a group, you must first give the group a name, then assign a password to the group. This is called *defining a group*.

Defining groups

You can establish a password for FileMaker Pro 3 files for use by a group. To define a group:

1. Choose *Define Groups* from the Access Privileges submenu in the File menu. The Define Groups dialog box appears.
2. In the Group Name box, type a name appropriate for the users of this database. You only need to give the access group a name and do not need to name each individual in that group.
3. Click the Done button when you are finished or choose the Passwords button to immediately set up a password for the group.

The Define Groups command is found under Access Privileges in the File menu.

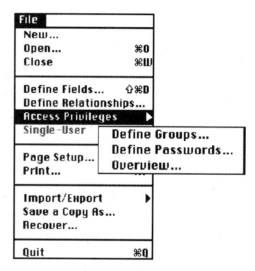

The buttons on the right-hand side of the Define Groups dialog box allow you to access the Passwords dialog box and the Access dialog box.

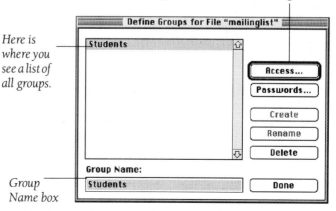

Here is where you see a list of all groups.

Group Name box

Access privileges

Good passwords

▲ *Do not include real words that can be found in the dictionary*

▲ *Should be a combination of numbers and letters*

▲ *Should not be written down where someone could find them*

▲ *Should be changed periodically*

Passwords

Good passwords are a combination of letters and numbers that do not make up actual words. This makes it harder for unauthorized users to figure out the password.

To create a password for a group:

1. Choose *Passwords* from the Access Privileges submenu in the File menu, or click Passwords in the Define Groups dialog box.

2. In the Privileges panel, select the activities you wish the users to be able to engage in. Your choices include:

▲ Access the entire file   ▲ Export records

▲ Browse records   ▲ Design layouts

▲ Print records   ▲ Edit scripts

▲ Create records   ▲ Define value list

▲ Edit records   ▲ Override data

▲ Delete records   entry warnings

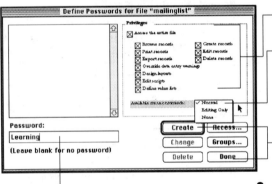

These checkboxes are where you select the activities you want the user to be able to engage in.

You can set this option so the user can both look at, enter, and edit information by changing the mode from Normal to Editing Only or None, which only lets users look at the information in the database.

Be sure to click the Create button before you click the Done button or your password is not saved.

This is where you type your password.

3. Select the menus you wish the user to be able to access from the Available menu commands pop-up list. Your choices include:

▲ Normal, which includes all menus

▲ Editing Only, which includes only the Edit menu

▲ None, which includes no available menus

4. In the Password box, type a password for the group or individual. You can see the password while you are typing it.

5. Click the Create button when you are finished assigning the password.

6. Click the Done button.

Using passwords

1. Open your password-protected file. The Password dialog box appears.
2. Type the correct password in the Password box. You cannot see the characters, you see just a line of dots.
3. Click the OK button when you are finished or press the Return key.

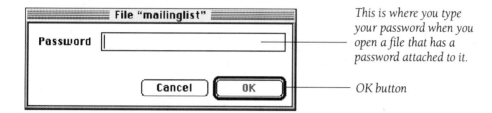

This is where you type your password when you open a file that has a password attached to it.

OK button

Incorrect passwords

What if you don't remember the password or you type the wrong password? A dialog box appears to tell you that you have typed the wrong password. The only thing you can do at that point is click the OK button.

Be sure to write down your password in a secure place, because if you don't remember it, you will not be able to access your file.

If you type your password incorrectly, this is the dialog box you see.

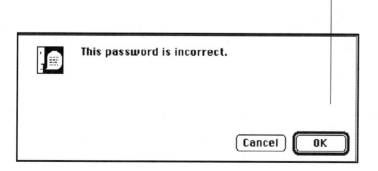

Access privileges

Access privileges

Overview

Overview shows you which groups have been set up, what the passwords for those groups are, how many layouts are in the database, and what the names are of all of the fields in the database.

To access the Overview command:

1. Choose *Overview* from the Access Privileges submenu in the File menu. The Access Privileges dialog box appears; *or*
Click the Access button from the Define Passwords or Define Groups dialog boxes.

2. Click the Done button when you are finished.

Groups contains the list of groups that have been defined. You can see the password for each group in the Passwords column.

Layouts lists the first layout and any other layouts this file contains. The Fields column lists the fields that make up this database.

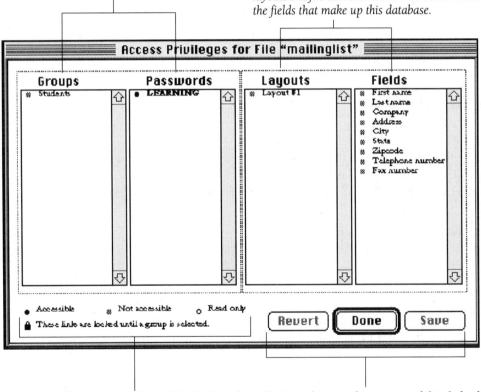

The Accessible, Not accessible, and Read only radio buttons tell you whether the user can open a file (Accessible), not open a file (Not accessible), or only look at a file (Read only).

The Done button takes you out of this dialog box. Save saves any changes, and Revert removes any recent changes and reverts the options back to the most recent saved version.

■ Changing data

After you create a database and enter data, you may want to add, change, copy, or delete some of the data in the fields.

Replacing information in a field

1. To replace all information in a single field, triple-click in that field.
2. Start typing the new information. The old information disappears.

Editing a field entry

1. Drag over the characters you wish to edit.
2. To replace the characters with new text, start typing the new information;
   or
   To delete the selected information, press the Delete key.

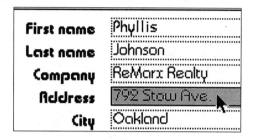

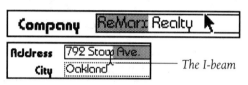

— *The I-beam*

✔ **Tip:** *When you triple-click in a field or when you drag over characters in a field, the selected area is highlighted. Dragging over characters turns the pointer into an I-beam. If you double-click in a field, you select the word you click on.*

Deleting information in a field

1. Triple-click the field you wish to erase.
2. Choose Clear from the Edit menu, or press the Clear key on the keyboard.

Undoing editing

▲ Immediately after making an editing mistake, choose Undo from the Edit menu, or press ⌘-**z**.

If you have typed anything or selected any other menu choice before you choose Undo, you will not be able to restore your editing changes.

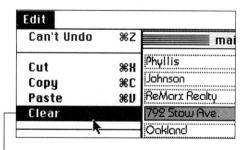

Clear on the Edit menu and the Clear key on the keyboard both delete all information within a field. If you make a mistake, choose Undo from the Edit menu. Notice the shortcut keys for Cut, Copy, and Paste on this menu.

Changing data

■ Cut and Copy

You can remove information or copy information in either a field or part of a field. For the various methods of deleting information, see the table below.

Cutting information

What you want to do	Action	Menu	Keys	Pastable
Delete characters in a field	Press Delete	None	Delete	No
Delete all information in a field	Press Clear	None	Clear	Undo with ⌘-z
Delete information in a field	Cut	Edit menu	⌘-x	Yes
Select all information in all fields to delete or copy it	Select All	Edit menu	⌘-A	Then cut or copy and paste

✔ Tip: *When you copy something with the Copy command, it is stored on the Macintosh Clipboard, and you can paste it as many times as you wish. When you copy a second piece of information, it replaces the first information you copied on the Clipboard. Now when you choose Paste, it will insert the second piece of information you copied.*

Copying and pasting information

1. Select the field you wish to copy.
2. Choose *Copy* from the Edit menu, or press ⌘-c.
3. Select the field where you want to place a copy of the information.
4. Choose *Paste* from the Edit menu, or press ⌘-v. The copied information immediately appears in the field.

✔ Tip: *You can copy information from one field and paste it into another field. You can also transfer information between records or databases by using the Cut and Paste commands.*

If you cut something you didn't mean to cut, you can use Undo to restore the information. See "Undoing editing" on page 19 for instructions in using Undo.

■ Duplicating a record

If you have a record you wish to copy exactly, you don't need to copy that record one field at a time—you can copy the entire record.

You might want to do this if you are creating records that are alike except for one field. First duplicate the record, then change that one field, rather than reentering the information or copying each field individually.

To duplicate a record:

1. Have the record you want to duplicate on the screen.
2. Choose *Duplicate Record* from the Mode menu, or press ⌘-**D**. An exact copy is made immediately.

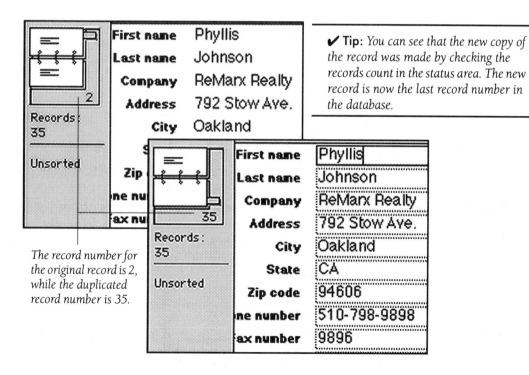

The record number for the original record is 2, while the duplicated record number is 35.

✔ **Tip:** *You can see that the new copy of the record was made by checking the records count in the status area. The new record is now the last record number in the database.*

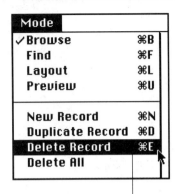

*Delete Record has a shortcut key, while the Delete
All command does not have a shortcut key. Be
careful when choosing Delete All records. Use this
option with Find to delete a found set of records,
for example, all people who live in California.*

■ Deleting a record

You can delete the current record you see on
screen, delete all records in the database, or delete
selected records.

Deleting the current record

1. Have the record you want to delete on the
   screen in front of you.
2. Choose *Delete Record* from the Mode menu,
   or press ⌘-**E**. The Delete record dialog
   box appears.
3. Click the Delete button if you want to delete
   this record;
   or
   Click the Cancel button if you don't wish to
   delete this record.

Deleting all records

1. Choose *Delete All* from the Mode menu. The
   Delete All records dialog box appears.
2. Click the Delete button if you want to delete
   these records;
   or
   Click the Cancel button if you don't wish to
   delete these records.

Deleting a found set of records

If you want to delete just some records, you first
need to select them. Find out how to select records
in "Finding records" on page 126. Then follow the
directions for deleting all records to delete the
selected records.

*When you choose to delete all records you see this
warning dialog box. Think about it, and if you
really mean to delete the records, go ahead and
click the Delete button. The warning box tells you
exactly how many records you are deleting.*

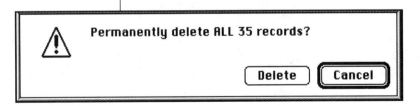

■ Using spelling checking

You can have spelling checked as you make entries in the fields, or you can check your spelling once all of the data entry is completed. Spelling options turn automatic spelling checking on or off.

Spelling options

1. Choose *Spelling Options* from the Spelling command on the Edit menu. The Spelling Options dialog box appears.

2. To have the computer beep when you type a misspelled word, select the Beep on questionable spellings radio button;
   or
   Select the Flash menu bar on questionable settings radio button to have the FileMaker Pro 3 menu bar flash when you type a misspelled word.

3. To turn spelling checking off, click the Off radio button.

4. Click the OK button.

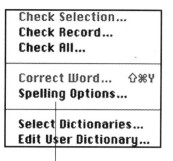

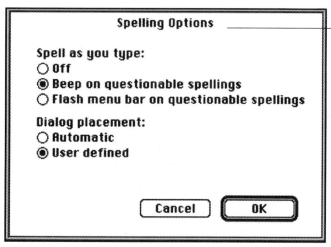

Checking the current record

1. Have the record you wish to check on the screen in front of you.

2. Choose *Check Record* from the Spelling submenu in the Edit menu. The Spelling dialog box appears. The first unknown word File-Maker Pro 3 finds appears in the Word box.

3. To replace the misspelled word, select the properly spelled word from the scrolling list and click the Replace button, or press the ⌘ key and the choice number.

4. To double-check the spelling, choose the Check button.

5. If the word is unique and not likely to be found in the dictionary, skip the word by choosing the Skip button.

6. If you are likely to use a unique word again and would like to add it to the user dictionary, click the Learn button.

7. To see a portion of the field that contains the misspelled word, click the Questionable Word pop-up list at the bottom of the Spelling dialog box.

8. Click the Done button;
    or
    Click the Cancel button if you wish to stop before the spelling checking is complete.

Spelling examples

Type of questionable spelling	Spelling action
Misspelled words such as *tihs* for *this*	Replace
Words you are not sure of such as *qualitative*	Check
Infrequently used words, special terms, or names, such as *quintessential*, *Lantastic*, or *Priddy*	Skip
Frequently used proper names, such as *ReMarx Realty*	Learn

There are two possible choices, indicated by ⌘-1 and ⌘-2.

Word box showing word with questionable spelling

When you are finished checking the spelling, the Replace button becomes a Done button.

Replace, Check, Skip, Learn, and Cancel buttons

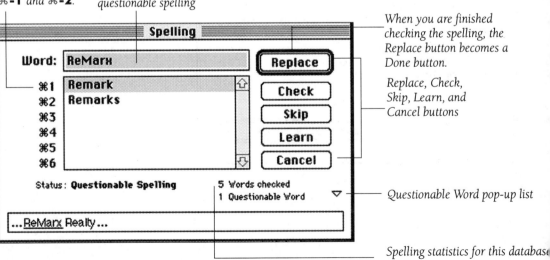

Questionable Word pop-up list

Spelling statistics for this database

Using spelling checking

Checking one word in a field

1. Have the record you wish to check on the screen in front of you.
2. Select the word in a field you wish to check.
3. Choose *Check Selection* from the Spelling submenu in the Edit menu. The Spelling dialog box appears.
4. Click either the Replace, Skip, or Learn options.
5. Click the Done button;
   or
   Click the Cancel button if you wish to cancel checking the word.

✔ **Tip:** *Don't forget—the Replace button becomes a Done button once checking the spelling has been completed. FileMaker Pro 3 determines automatically when it has finished checking a file, record, or word.*

Changing dictionaries

1. Choose *Select Dictionaries* from the Spelling submenu in the Edit menu. The Select Dictionaries dialog box appears.
2. Select the dictionary type, either Main Dictionary or User Dictionary from the Select Dictionary Type pop-up menu.
3. Choose the location of the new dictionary from the location pop-up menu.
4. When the dictionary name appears in the scrolling box, select the name, and click the Open button.
5. Click the Done button when you are finished.

Ah those changing buttons! Frequently a button will change functions entirely once you have selected an item or performed an action. This time the Select button changes to the Open button once you have clicked a dictionary.

There are two types of dictionaries you can install—main dictionaries and user dictionaries. Main dictionaries are full dictionaries, while user dictionaries are lists of words that have been added using the Learn button in the spelling dialog box.

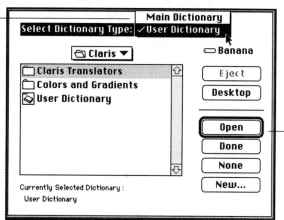

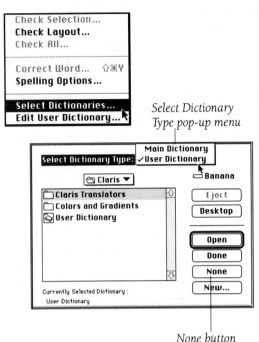

Select Dictionary
Type pop-up menu

None button

Turning user dictionaries off

1. Choose *Select Dictionaries* from the Spelling submenu in the Edit menu. The Select Dictionaries dialog box appears.
2. Choose *User Dictionary* from the Select Dictionary Type pop-up menu.
3. Choose the user dictionary from the scrolling box.
4. Click the None button.
5. Click the Done button.

✔ **Tip:** *You cannot edit an entry in the user dictionary directly. First remove the entry, then add the entry back in, being careful to type it correctly in the Entry box.*

The words appear as a simple scrolling list.

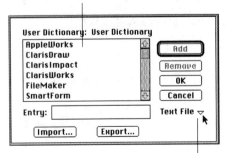

Use the Text File button to activate the Import and Export buttons.

Editing the user dictionary

The user dictionary contains words you have added with the Learn option from the Spelling dialog box.

To edit the user dictionary:

1. Choose *Edit User Dictionary* from the Spelling submenu in the Edit menu. The Edit User Dictionary dialog box appears.
2. Select the word you wish to remove and click the Remove button;
   or
   Type a new word in the Entry box and click the Add button;
   or
   Click the Text File button to import a spelling list or to export the spelling list as a text file.
3. Click the OK button when you are finished.

Layouts & parts

■ FileMaker Pro 3 layouts

FileMaker Pro 3 provides seven layout types that let you control screen appearance and determine how your database prints out. Your database can have as many different layouts as you wish.

Layout screen

Here is a sample layout, complete with all of the elements you would find in most layouts. Notice the parts that divide the layout into sections, and the changes in the tools on the left-hand side of the screen.

Special fields—This is a date field. Other special fields include page number or record number.

Text and graphics—Both can be added to a layout. This layout has a typed title surrounded by a drawn box that is filled with black.

Layouts menu

Status area showing that this layout is layout number 5 out of 5 layouts

Layout tools— These tools draw shapes and buttons, and create portals to help you view information from other databases.

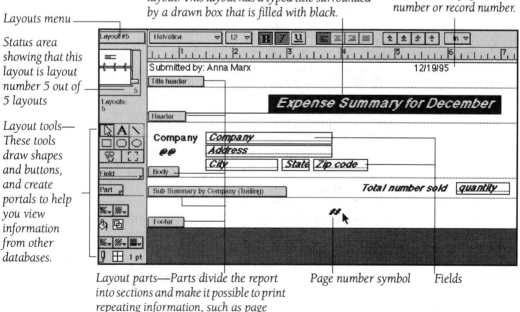

Layout parts—Parts divide the report into sections and make it possible to print repeating information, such as page numbers, or to summarize data.

Page number symbol

Fields

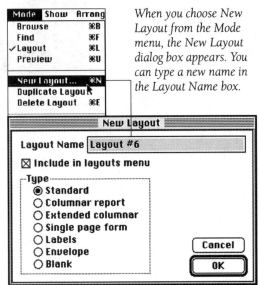

When you choose New Layout from the Mode menu, the New Layout dialog box appears. You can type a new name in the Layout Name box.

Setting up a new layout

1. Choose *Layout* from the Mode menu, or press ⌘-**L**. The layout screen appears.
2. Choose *New Layout* from the Mode menu, or press ⌘-**N**. The New Layout dialog box appears.
3. In the Layout Name box, type a new name for the layout. The default name tells you what number this layout is.
4. Select the type of layout from the Type panel radio buttons.
5. Click the OK button when you are finished.

Layout types

There are seven layout types in the Type panel of the New Layout dialog box. Make the report type selection based on the characteristics described in the table below. See "Labels and envelopes" on page 31 for specific information.

Report types

Report type	Default characteristics	Field orientation
Standard	Single 8 1/2" by 11" page containing all fields and Header, Body, and Footer parts	Vertical
Columnar report	Single 8 1/2" by 11" page in two columns—secondary menu lets you choose which fields can be included	Vertical
Extended columnar	Single page of variable width	Horizontal
Single page form	Single 8 1/2" by 11" page containing all fields—contains only a Body part, no subparts	Vertical
Labels	Avery label numbers or custom labels—secondary menu lets you choose which fields can be included and where they are placed	Vertical
Envelope	Standard #10 envelope—secondary menu lets you choose which fields can be included and where they are placed	Vertical
Blank	Contains no fields, but contains Header, Body, and Footer parts	None

Changing a layout name

If you forgot to give the layout a unique name when you first set it up, you can give it a name later.

To change a layout name:

1. Choose *Layout Setup* from the Mode menu. The Layout Setup dialog box appears.

2. Type a new layout name in the Layout Name box.

3. Click the OK button.

✔ **Tip:** *If you have a report that you don't want to show in the layouts menu, deselect the Include in layouts menu checkbox.*

Layout Setup dialog box—this box is where you change:

▲ *The layout name*

▲ *Whether to include the layout in the layouts menu*

▲ *Whether you want to print in columns*

▲ *How many columns you want to print on a page*

▲ *Whether the columns should print across or down the page*

▲ *What the page margins should be*

▲ *Whether you want the report to print on facing pages*

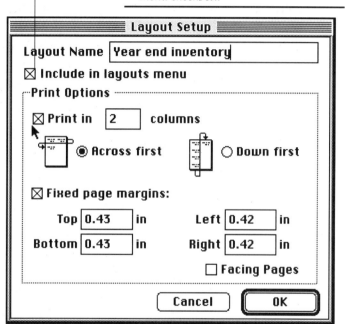

Layout Setup

Layout Name │Year end inventory│

☒ **Include in layouts menu**

Print Options

☒ **Print in** │2│ **columns**

⊙ **Across first**   ○ **Down first**

☒ **Fixed page margins:**

Top │0.43│ in   Left │0.42│ in

Bottom │0.43│ in   Right │0.42│ in

☐ **Facing Pages**

[Cancel]   [OK]

Printing in columns

Whether or not your report was designated a columnar report, if the report is narrow enough, you can print it out in columns:

1. Choose *Layout Setup* from the Mode menu. The Layout Setup dialog box appears.

2. Select the Print in checkbox option in the Print Options panel.

3. In the columns box, type the number of columns you want your page to have.

4. Select the proper orientation radio button, either Across first or Down first.

5. Click the OK button.

FileMaker Pro 3 layouts

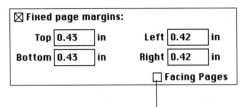

Use Facing Pages when you want to create a report that is printed on both sides of the paper and bound in the center. When you select this checkbox, the Left and Right margins are called Inside and Outside margins.

Page margins

If the default page margins are not exactly what you had in mind, you can change them.

1. Choose *Layout Setup* from the Mode menu. The Layout Setup dialog box appears.

2. Select the Fixed page margins checkbox.

3. Type the first margin you want in the Top margin box.

4. Tap the Tab key to move to the next margin. Finish entering the proper margins for all four margins.

5. Click the OK button.

Note: The smallest margin you can type is determined by the type of printer you are using. Printers cannot usually print right out to the very edge of the paper.

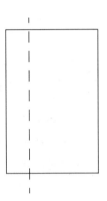

Left margin without the Facing Pages box selected

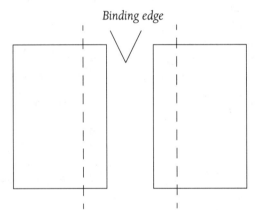

When you select Facing Pages, the left margin (on the right-hand page) becomes the Inside margin on both the right- and left-hand pages.

FileMaker Pro 3 layouts

■ Labels and envelopes

Choose your layout type carefully before you begin placing fields; you cannot change the layout type once you have entered the layout screen.

Labels

1. Choose *Layout* from the Mode menu, or press ⌘-L. The layout screen appears.
2. Choose *New Layout* from the Mode menu, or press ⌘-N. The New Layout dialog box appears.
3. In the Layout Name box, type a new name for the layout. The default name tells you what number this layout is.
4. Select the Label radio button from the Type panel.
5. Click the OK button. The Label Setup dialog box appears.
6. Select the Use label measurements radio button if it is not already selected.
7. Select the Avery label type from the labels pop-up list. The Specify Layout Contents dialog box appears.
8. Double-click the first field you want to appear on the label. The field name appears within the Layout contents box.
9. Press the Return key to start a new line and enter the next field(s) you want to appear on the label.

Note: The Layout contents box determines the placement of the fields. You can either type in any punctuation you need between fields, or you can select the punctuation from the punctuation buttons on the top of the screen.

10. Click the OK button when you are finished.

When the layout appears with the field names surrounded by double brackets, you can see gray areas for the other blank labels that fit across the page.

Use the labels pop-up list to select the Avery label type. You don't need to buy Avery brand labels; all labels give an Avery size number.

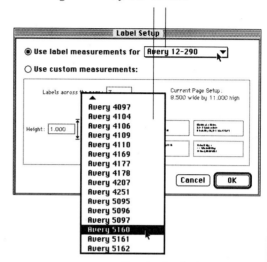

Punctuation buttons

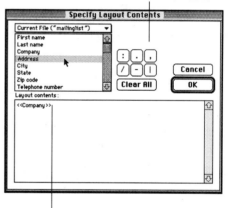

Think of the Layout contents box as a sample label. The fields appear surrounded by double brackets <<like this>>.

If you make a mistake, remove all of the fields in the Layout contents box by clicking the Clear All button, or select the field name, including the double brackets, and tap the Delete key.

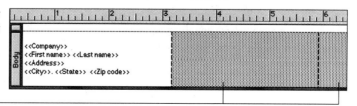

Envelopes

1. Choose *Layout* from the Mode menu, or press ⌘-L. The layout screen appears.
2. Choose *New Layout* from the Mode menu, or press ⌘-N. The New Layout dialog box appears.
3. In the Layout Name box, type a new name for the layout. The default name tells you what number this layout is.
4. Select the Envelope radio button from the Type panel.
5. Click the OK button. The Specify Layout Contents dialog box appears.
6. Double-click the first field you want to appear on the envelope. The field name appears within the Layout contents box.
7. Press the Return key to start a new line and enter the next field(s) you want to appear on the label.
8. Click the OK button.

—Placement of the address on the layout depends on how the Page Setup dialog box is filled out. Each printer has a slightly different dialog box.

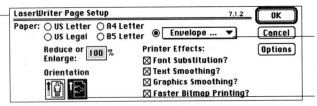

— Here is where Envelope is selected.

Here is where the envelope orientation is selected.

Envelopes and printers

Now that you have your fields selected, you need to make the envelope work with your printer:

1. In the Layout mode, choose *Page Setup* from the File menu.
2. Select the Envelope paper type for your printer. This sample shows how you select the paper type for a LaserWriter printer.
3. Change the Orientation button if you need to. For laser printers, the Orientation button should be landscape or wide.
4. Click the OK button.
5. In the layout, select and drag the fields into proper position within the Body part.

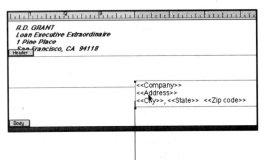

✔ **Tip:** *If you turn on the graphic rulers, you can see exactly where you drag the fields. Turn on the graphic rulers using the Show menu.*

Creating a return address

1. In the Envelope layout, select the text tool (the button with the A on it) from the toolbox.
2. Type your return address above the Header part, changing the font, font size, and style if you need to.
3. Drag the Header divider line close to the bottom of the return address.
4. Drag the return address if you need to reposition it.

A part division shows up as a dotted line with a part label on the left-hand side of the layout. When the pointer is on top of the divider, it appears as a double-sided pointer.

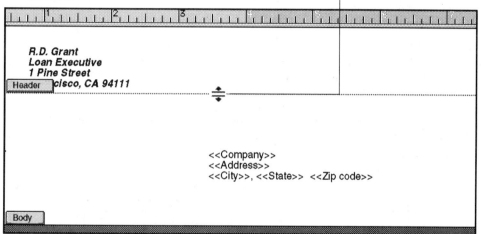

Labels and envelopes

To see the envelope

▲ Choose *Preview* from the Mode menu to see an envelope.

▲ Click the minimize button from the bottom toolbar to change the view so you can see the entire envelope.

Click here to see the entire envelope on the computer screen.

Envelope with return address as seen in the Preview mode, zoomed out to 50 percent

R.D. Grant
Loan Executive
1 Pine St.
San Francisco, CA 94110

Jordan Bright
1 Market Plaza
San Francisco, CA 94110

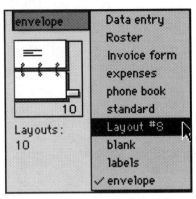

Select the layout you want to delete from the layouts menu.

■ Removing layouts

If you have a layout you no longer want, you can delete the layout:

1. Using the layouts menu, switch to the layout you wish to delete.
2. Choose *Layout* from the Mode menu.
3. Choose *Delete Layout*, or press ⌘-**E**. The Delete Layout dialog box appears.
4. Click the Delete button to delete the layout, or click the Cancel button to stop this operation.

There's that double-sided pointer again. Every time you move something you'll see it.

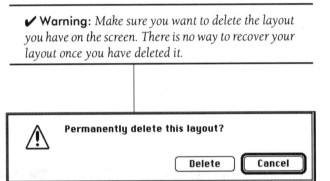

✔ **Warning:** *Make sure you want to delete the layout you have on the screen. There is no way to recover your layout once you have deleted it.*

■ Reordering the layouts menu

If you don't like the order in which the layouts appear in the layouts menu, you can change it:

1. Choose *Layout* from the Mode menu.
2. Choose *Set Layout Order* from the Mode menu. The Set Layout Order dialog box appears.
3. Drag the layout you wish to change to the proper position.
4. If you want to exclude a layout from the menu, deselect the Include in layouts menu checkbox.
5. Click the OK button.

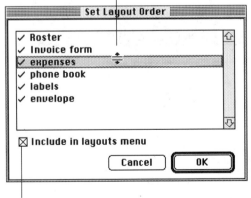

You can remove a layout from the layouts menu by deselecting the Include in layouts menu checkbox.

■ Adding parts

The purpose of parts

Layouts contain parts that control how information appears in the data entry form. Typical parts include the body, headers, or footers.

Adding parts—Method 1

1. In the Layout mode, drag the Part button on the left-hand side of the toolbox to the proper position on the layout. The Part Definition dialog box appears.
2. Select the part type radio button.
3. Click the OK button.

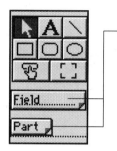

The Field and Part buttons can be used in the Layout mode and are located in the toolbox on the left-hand side of the screen.

To use them, drag the appropriate button on top of the layout.

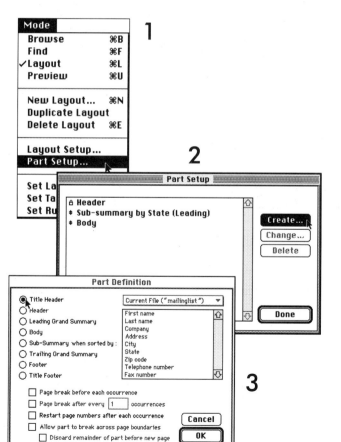

Adding parts—Method 2

1. In the Layout mode, choose *Part Setup* from the Mode menu. The Part Setup dialog box appears.
2. Click the Create button in the Part Setup dialog box. The Part Definition dialog box appears.
3. Select the radio button for the type of part you wish to create, and click the OK button.
4. Click the Done button. The new part appears in the most logical position on the layout.

✔ **Warning:** *If the part you wish to delete contains any fields, those fields also are deleted. There is no warning when you press the Delete button—your part disappears quite quickly.*

Once you select the part you want to delete, a Delete button appears on the right side of the Part Setup dialog box.

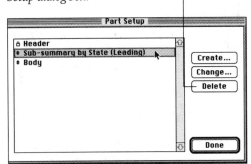

You are warned that all of the fields, lines, and other information in this part will be deleted at the same time.

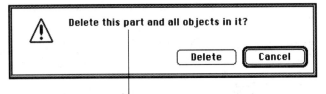

■ Deleting parts

Deleting parts—Method 1

1. In the Layout mode, select the label for the part you wish to delete. Make sure there are no fields, text, or graphics in this part.
2. Press the Delete key.

Deleting parts—Method 2

1. In the Layout mode, select the part you wish to delete.
2. Choose *Part Setup* from the Mode menu. The Part Setup dialog box appears.
3. Select the part you wish to delete from the scrolling list.
4. Click the Delete button in the Part Setup dialog box. The Delete this part dialog box appears.
5. Click the Delete button to delete the part; *or* Click the Cancel button to stop this operation.

■ Part attributes

The Part Definition dialog box also contains a group of checkboxes for selecting the part's attributes. These attributes include:

▲ Page break before each occurrence, which places a page break just before each occurrence of that part.

▲ Page break after every [number of] occurrences, which places a page break just after *x* number of occurrences of that layout part. You specify the number of occurrences in the occurrences box.

▲ Restart page numbers after each occurrence, which starts the page numbers over at 1 when this part is reached.

▲ Allow part to break across page boundaries, which allows the contents of a part to occupy more than one page.

▲ Discard remainder of part before new page, which prints as much of a field in any given part as fits on the bottom of a page. The rest of the field is not printed.

Changing part attributes

1. In the Layout mode, double-click the part you wish to change. The Part Definition dialog box appears.
2. Select the checkboxes for the part attributes you wish to use.
3. Click the OK button.

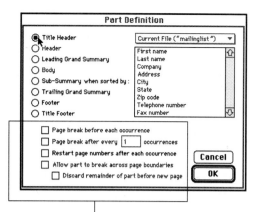

These are the part attributes. To use any attribute, just select the checkbox.

✔ **Tip:** *You can also access the Part Definition dialog box with the Part Setup command in the Mode menu.*

■ Top of the page parts

Title Header and regular Header parts go at the top of the page.

Creating headers

1. In the Layout mode, drag the Part button on the left-hand side of the toolbox to a position near the top of the layout. The Part Definition dialog box appears.

2. Select the Title Header or Header part type radio button.

3. Click the OK button when you are finished.

To get your part into the correct position, drag it to where it belongs in the parts order list. Title headers and headers go at the top of the layout.

Drag the Part button in the toolbox to your layout in this direction to place a Header or Title Header part correctly.

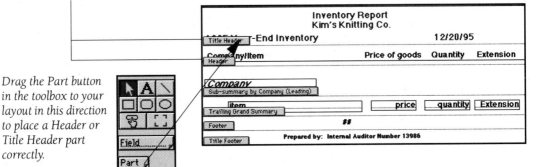

Layout Part Order

Location on report	Part name	Function
Top	Title Header	Appears only on first page
	Header	Appears on all other pages
	Leading Grand Summary	Used to group information
Middle	Body	Contains repeating or main information
Bottom	Sub-Summary when sorted by	Used to summarize subsections of information, such as a subtotal
	Trailing Grand Summary	Used to summarize all information, such as a grand total
	Footer	Appears on all pages except the first page when you have a title header
	Title Footer	Appears only on the first page

■ Body parts

Body parts are used for main information such as items, addresses, and description information.

Body parts can also be used for repeating information. For example, if you are creating an invoice and you realize you might sell more than one item to a customer, the field for items can be placed in the Body part more than once.

The Body part is a default part for all layouts except the Blank layout type.

To create a Body part:

1. In the Layout mode, drag the Part button on the left-hand side of the toolbox to a position near the middle of the layout. The Part Definition dialog box appears.

2. Select the Body part type radio button.

3. Click the OK button.

This finished invoice form uses the Body part to hold the item, quantity, price, and extension fields. The address information is in the Header, and the total due field is in a Trailing Grand Summary part.

For information on how to create repeating fields like this invoice sample, see "Repeating fields" on page 54.

Parts are marked by a tag on the left-hand side of the page and a dotted line extending to the right.

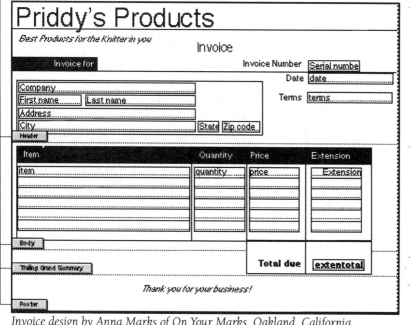

Header part *contains the company name, invoice number, and customer address information because this information occurs only once in an invoice.*

Body part *contains item, quantity, price, and extension information. These fields are repeating fields and occur more than once.*

Trailing Grand Summary *contains a field that adds up all of the extensions.*

Footer *contains footer information.*

Invoice design by Anna Marks of On Your Marks, Oakland, California

Body parts

■ Parts for math and sorting

Summary parts help you group information together then obtain subtotals and totals on that information.

Leading grand summary

Leading grand summaries use summary fields to place total calculations at the beginning of a report.

Sub-Summary when sorted by...

Leading sub-summaries group information by a particular field, for example, salesperson, state, or company.

Leading sub-summaries require the field that is used to group the information to be sorted before this report works.

This sub-summary part occurs at the top of a report and groups information by the Company field. Before this report previews or prints out correctly, the Company field must be sorted. For information on sorting, see "Sorting" on page 121.

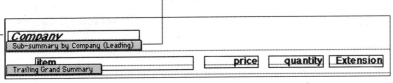

Notice that the field appears above the part label.

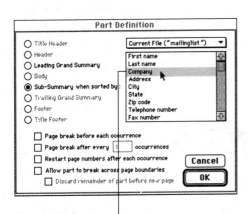

Select the field you want to group your information on from this scrolling list.

Creating a leading sub-summary

1. In the Layout mode, drag the Part button on the left-hand side of the toolbox to a position near the top of the layout. The Part Definition dialog box appears.
2. Select the Sub-Summary when sorted by radio button.
3. Select the field you want to group your information by from the scrolling list on the right-hand side of the Part Definition dialog box.
4. Click the OK button.
5. Place the field you selected from the scrolling list just above the part label.

Trailing sub-summaries

Trailing sub-summaries use summary fields to place subtotal calculations at the end of a report.

Trailing grand summaries

Trailing grand summaries use summary fields to place grand total calculations at the end of a report. Both the Trailing Grand Summary and sub-summary fields are created the same way.

The Body part contains extension fields that need to be added up for a final total.

The Trailing Grand Summary part contains the calculating field that adds together all of the extension fields in the Body part.

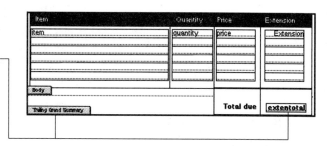

Creating a sub-summary calculation field

1. In the Layout mode, drag the Part button on the left-hand side of the toolbox to a position near the top of the layout. The Part Definition dialog box appears.
2. Select the Trailing Grand Summary radio button.
3. Click the OK button.
4. Choose *Define Fields* from the File menu, or press ⇧⌘-**D**. The Define Fields dialog box appears.
5. Type a name for the summary field in the Field Name box.
6. Select the Summary radio button from the Type panel of the Define Fields dialog box, or press ⌘-**S**.
7. Click the Create button. The Options for Summary Field dialog box appears.
8. Select the radio button for the type of math you want performed in the sub-summary calculation field.
9. Select the summary field from the scrolling list on the right-hand side of the dialog box.
10. Click the OK button.
11. Click the Done button in the Define Fields dialog box.

The radio buttons determine the type of calculation this sub-summary performs.

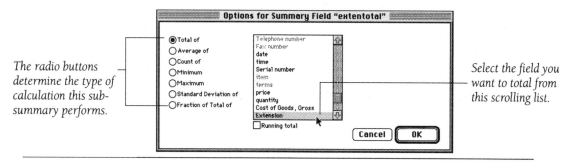

Select the field you want to total from this scrolling list.

■ Bottom of the page parts

Regular footers and title footers work just like headers—title footers appear on the first page only and regular footers appear on all of the other pages.

Creating a footer

1. In the Layout mode, drag the Part button on the left-hand side of the toolbox to a position near the bottom of the layout. The Part Definition dialog box appears.
2. Select the Title Footer or Footer part type radio button.
3. Click the OK button.

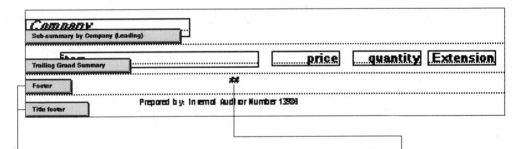

The order parts appear in is important. Notice that the Title Footer appears after the regular Footer. Similarly, a Title Header appears first in a layout, with the regular Header second.

The double hash symbol (##) is a special code indicating the position for page numbers. FileMaker Pro 3 then places the correct page number in that position. To find out about pasting special symbols in, see "Paste Special commands" on page 44.

■ Page breaks

You can determine where page breaks occur in your layouts. To insert a page break into a form:

1. Choose *Part Setup* from the Mode menu. The Part Setup dialog box occurs.

2. Select the part that marks where you want the page break to start. In the example below, I used the leading sub-summary part.

3. Click the Change button. The Part Definition dialog box appears.

4. Select the Page break before each occurrence checkbox.

5. Click the OK button. The Print Above/Print Below dialog box appears.

6. Click the Print Above or Print Below button.
▲ Print Above causes the field that is in the part you have chosen to print at the top of the page.
▲ Print Below causes the field that is in the part you have chosen to print at the bottom of the page.

7. Click the Done button.

This dialog box determines whether or not the field prints at the top of the page or at the end of the records. The example below prints at the top of the page (Print Above).

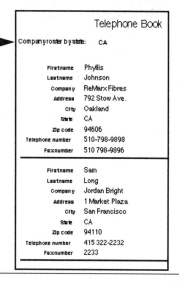

⚠ **This part can be printed aboue or below the records that it summarizes.**

[Cancel]   [**Print Aboue**]
[**Print Below**]

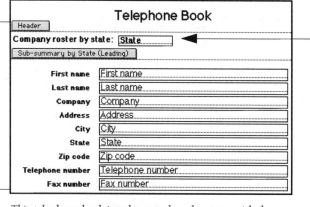

This telephone book is to be sorted out by state, with the state printing at the top of the page. Every time a new state appears, a page break occurs. Sorting keeps all of the entries for one state together.

Page breaks

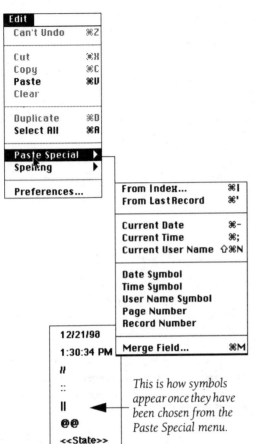

This is how symbols appear once they have been chosen from the Paste Special menu.

■ Paste Special commands

Some information doesn't have to have a field created for it—it's already contained in FileMaker Pro 3. The Paste Special command allows you to insert information such as:

▲ Information carried over from the previous record

▲ Current date or time

▲ Current user name

▲ Date, time, or user symbols

▲ Page number

▲ Record number

▲ Merge field

To use a Paste Special command:

1. In the Layout mode, choose *Paste Special* from the Edit menu. A submenu appears.

2. Select the special symbol you want to paste from the Paste Special submenu. The symbol appears on the layout.

3. Move the symbol to the proper position by dragging it.

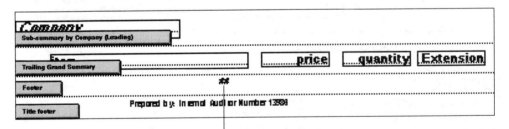

Here the Page Number command was used from the Paste Special menu. The symbol is placed in the Footer so the page number prints on every page.

✔ **Tip:** *The Current Date command in the Paste Special menu pastes in today's date. It will always be whatever that date is in your layout. The Date Symbol command, however, checks and updates your layout to show you the current date.*

■ Moving the part labels

Those pesky part labels often extend out over the layout so you can't really work well (see illustration on the left, below). You can move the part labels over to the left and arrange them so that they display vertically.

There is only one small drawback when you move the part labels so they display vertically—you might not be able to read the part label. There's a cure for that too!

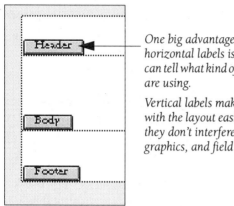

One big advantage of horizontal labels is that you can tell what kind of a part you are using.

Vertical labels make working with the layout easier because they don't interfere with text, graphics, and field placement.

Making vertical part labels

▲ In the Layout mode, click the mode selector in the bottom toolbar.

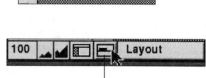

In the Layout mode, click here to make the labels display vertically. To return them to the horizontal state, just click the button again.

Seeing the part label name

▲ Double-click the vertical part label and the Part Definition dialog box appears. You can then see what type of part you are working with, or you can make changes to that part.

Remember this dialog box? The radio buttons show you what kind of part you are working with. For more information on defining parts, see "Adding parts" on page 35.

Part Definition

- ◉ Title Header
- ○ Header
- ○ Leading Grand Summary
- ○ Body
- ○ Sub-Summary when sorted by :
- ○ Trailing Grand Summary
- ○ Footer
- ○ Title Footer

Current File ("mailinglist") ▼

First name
Last name
Company
Address
City
State
Zip code
Telephone number
Fax number

- ☐ Page break before each occurrence
- ☐ Page break after every 1 occurrences
- ☐ Restart page numbers after each occurrence
- ☐ Allow part to break across page boundaries
- ☐ Discard remainder of part before new page

[Cancel]
[OK]

Moving the part labels

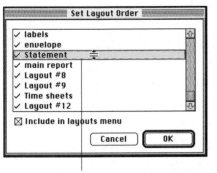

Select the field and drag it into the correct position in the list.

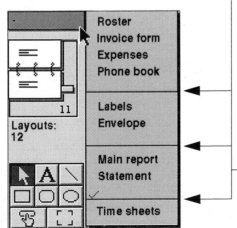

■ Changing the layouts menu order

Initially, the layouts appear in the layouts menu in the order they are created. You aren't stuck with this. You can move them around and create your own order on the menu.

To change the order of items in the layouts menu:

1. In the Layout mode, choose *Set Layout Order* from the Mode menu. The Set Layout Order dialog box appears.

2. Select the layout you wish to change and drag it up (or down) the list until it is in the proper position. Notice that the cursor becomes a double-sided arrow.

3. Click the OK button.

Subdividing the layouts menu

Horizontal rule divisions are a nice little piece of window dressing for the layouts menu.

To subdivide the layouts menu:

1. In the Layout mode, create as many blank layouts (with no fields) as you want dividers.

2. In each of these new layouts, choose *Layout Setup* from the Mode menu. The Layout Setup dialog box appears.

3. Type a simple hyphen (-) for the Layout name.

4. Click the OK button when you are finished.

5. Still in the Layout mode, choose *Set Layout Order* from the Mode menu. The Set Layout Order dialog box appears.

6. Select the Layout with the hyphen (-) for a name and drag it up (or down) the list until it is in the proper position.

7. Click the OK button.

Make your layouts menu easier to use by dividing the items on it into functional groups.

■ Sample layout

This recipe layout gives the parts a real workout! We've detailed how we created the layout, including the math you need to make it work here for you.

Recipe database—the recipes

Each recipe gets a nice data entry form that can be printed out to form a book—but the real trick comes when we create the index.

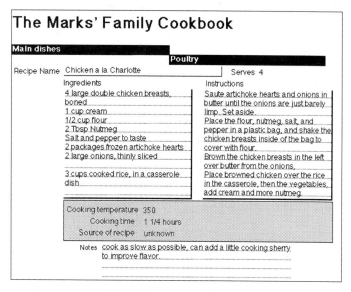

Lots of parts make this database easy to organize!

▲ *The Header part contains the running header and title of the cookbook.*

▲ *Sub-summary by Type of Recipe (leading) organizes the main categories, such as Main dishes, Desserts, Salads. This field needs to be sorted to make this layout work.*

▲ *Sub-summary by Category of Recipe (leading) is the second leading summary that sorts out the recipe by a subdivision of Type of Recipe, as in Main dishes—Poultry, Main dishes—Beef, and so on.*

▲ *Body contains the recipe information.*

▲ *Footer could contain page numbers, dates, and so on.*

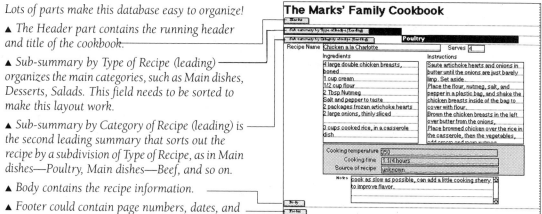

Recipe database—the index

We used page numbers just in case two recipes print on one piece of paper. The page numbers are from the *Paste Special* submenu in the Edit menu. We also created this layout after the Recipe main layout—we simply copied the layout and deleted the body.

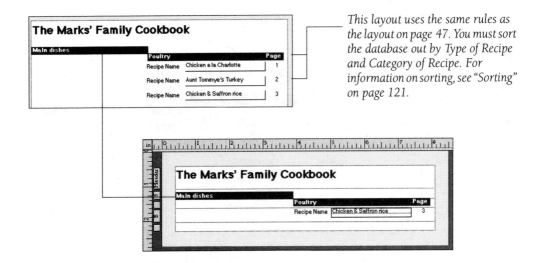

This layout uses the same rules as the layout on page 47. You must sort the database out by Type of Recipe and Category of Recipe. For information on sorting, see "Sorting" on page 121.

Sample layout

Working with fields

◼ Creating fields

After you have created your database and defined the fields, you might want to add, change, or delete fields.

You can define a field while you are in the Browse mode or the Layout mode.

Adding fields

1. Choose *Define Fields* from the File menu, or press ⇧⌘-**D**. The Define Fields dialog box appears.
2. Select the field type you want by choosing the corresponding radio button in the Type panel.
3. Type a field name in the Field Name box.
4. Click the Create button.
5. Click the Done button in the Define Fields dialog box. The field and field label appear on the layout.

Deleting fields

1. Choose *Define Fields* from the File menu, or press ⇧⌘-**D**. The Define Fields dialog box appears.
2. In the Field Name list, select the name of the field you wish to delete.
3. Click the Delete button. A warning box appears.
4. Click the Delete button in the warning box.
5. Click the Done button in the Define Fields dialog box.

Remember to select the correct radio button for the type of field you want to create.

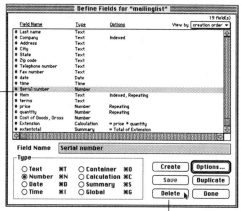

When you select a field from the scrolling list, the Delete button is available for use. All information that was in the field is deleted.

When you want to change a name, just edit the name in the Field Name box—but be sure to click the Save button to save the new name.

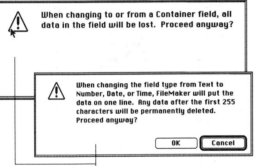

Two typical warning messages that can occur when you change field types. Be sure to read the contents carefully. The exact message depends on the type of change you wish to make.

Changing field definitions

Field definitions include the Field Name, Type, and Options.

To change the field name

1. Choose *Define Fields* from the File menu, or press ⇧⌘-**D**. The Define Fields dialog box appears.
2. In the Field Name list, select the name of the field you wish to change.
3. Make the changes to the field name in the Field Name box, then click the Save button.
4. Click the Done button.

Changing Field types

1. Choose *Define Fields* from the File menu, or press ⇧⌘-**D**. The Define Fields dialog box appears.
2. In the Field Name list, select the name of the field you wish to change.
3. Select the Type radio button you wish to use.
4. Click the Save button to save this change. A warning box may appear. Read the message carefully and if you still want to make the change, click the OK button in the warning box, or click the Cancel button if you don't want to go through with the change.
5. Click the Done button.

✔ **Warning:** *Sometimes when you change field types, the new definition does not work with existing data. When this happens, FileMaker Pro 3 displays an error dialog box. Depending on the nature of the change, the error dialog box lets you know what happens to any existing data.*

■ Types of data

The Type panel of the Define Fields dialog box gives you eight choices. Text and Number are explained in "Type of information" on page 3. Here is how you work with the other types of information.

Date or time fields

1. Choose *Define Fields* from the File menu, or press ⇧⌘-**D**. The Define Fields dialog box appears.
2. Choose either the Date or Time radio button in the Type panel of the Define Fields dialog box.
3. Type a name in the Field Name box.
4. Click the Create button.
5. Click the Done button when you are finished.

This is how the date and time fields appear in the scrolling list of the Define Fields dialog box.

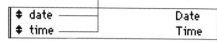

This is how the date and time fields appear in the database itself on the data entry form.

✔ **Note:** *Both the Date and Time field types must be formatted later to display the information in a format you desire. For example, you can make the date display as 1/1/97 or January 1, 1997. There are multiple options for displaying the time also. Formatting fields is discussed in "Formatting data types" on page 74.*

Types of data

✔ **Note:** *If you change a field to an Auto Enter field and the database already has records in it, the new Auto Enter options work only with new records and do not affect previously entered information.*

■ Auto Enter data

With the Auto Enter capability, FileMaker Pro 3 can automatically enter serial numbers for invoices, current dates, or other automatic information.

To use Auto Enter:

1. Choose *Define Fields* from the File menu, or press ⇧⌘-**D**. The Define Fields dialog box appears.
2. Create the field you want to use with Auto Enter, following steps 2 through 4 in "Adding fields" on page 49.
3. Once you have created the field name and field type, click the Options button. The Entry Options dialog box appears.

The Entry Options pop-up menu

These seven radio buttons determine the type of automatically entered data. Some of the buttons require a second step in the layout itself to make them work properly, for example the Calculated value and Looked-up value radio buttons.

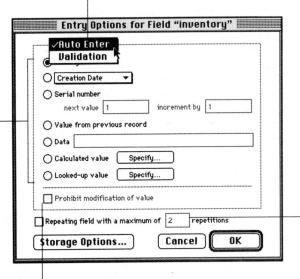

Repeating fields are great for creating invoice forms where a variety of sales information is entered for one customer.

✔ **Tip:** *If you don't want the user to be able to change automatically entered data, at the bottom of the Auto Enter panel check the box labeled Prohibit modification of value to prevent any changes being made to this field.*

4. The pop-up menu at the top of the dialog box should say Auto Enter. If it does not, choose Auto Enter from this pop-up menu.
5. Select one of the seven radio buttons in the Auto Enter selection panel.
6. Click the OK button.
7. Click the Done button in the Define Fields dialog box.

■ Auto Enter data types

Determining which radio button to select can be tricky. Use the following chart to help you.

Auto Enter data types

Auto Enter type	Type of action performed	Additional steps
Nothing	Turns off Auto Enter options.	None. Automatically entered text is converted to plain text.
Creation date pop-up menu	Enters creation date and time, modification date and time, or creator or modifier name.	Date and time data may need to be formatted. See "Formatting text fields" on page 74.
Serial number	Lets you start with any number and increase each new entry by any number.	Make sure you start with the first number you want to use and you type in the correct "step," or amount for the numbers to increase each time.
Value from previous record	Copies whatever was entered in this field on previous record.	None—and it sure is quicker than copy and paste.
Data	Enters data typed in the data entry box in this field.	Type what you would like to have entered in your database for this field.
Calculated value	Creates a calculation based on other fields.	For more information about calculations, see "Creating basic calculations" on page 108.
Looked-up value	Lets you borrow information from other databases.	For more information on borrowing data, see "Using a related field" on page 156.

Auto Enter data types

■ Additional Auto Enter options

Several useful options are available on the bottom of the Entry Options dialog box. These include repeating fields and storage options.

Repeating fields

Repeating fields can be used when you need more than one occurrence of a field in a layout.

The example to the left shows an invoice form that has repeating fields for the items the customer is ordering.

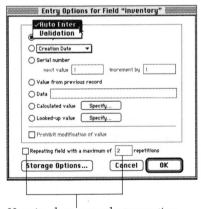

Repeating fields share characteristics such as font, font size, format, and alignment. To change the width of any repeating field, just drag the top field in the group to the proper shape and the rest will follow.

Here is where you select repeating fields and type in the number of repetitions you want to use.

To create a repeating field:

1. Choose *Define Fields* from the File menu, or press ⇧⌘-**D**. The Define Fields dialog box appears.

2. Create the field you want to use with Auto Enter, following steps 2 through 4 in "Adding fields" on page 49.

3. Once you have created the field name and field type, click the Options button. The Entry Options dialog box appears.

4. Select the Repeating field with a maximum of box and type the number of repeated fields you want in the repetitions box.

5. Click the OK button in the Entry Options dialog box.

6. Click the Done button in the Define Fields dialog box.

Formatting a repeating field

Once you have created the repeating field in the Define Fields dialog box, you must format it:

1. In the Layout mode, select the repeating field. You should see only one instance of that field the first time you look at it.
2. Choose *Field Format* from the Format menu, or press Option-⌘-**F**. The Field Format dialog box appears.
3. In the Field Format dialog box, type the number of repetitions you wish the field to have in this layout.
4. Select either vertical or horizontal orientation from the orientation pop-up list.
5. Click the OK button.

✔ **Note:** *If you need more repetitions than the Repetitions panel says you have, go back to the Define Fields dialog box, click the Options button in the Entry Options dialog box, and enter a larger number in the repetitions box.*

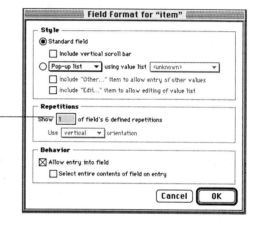

Here is where you type in the number of repetitions you want in your layout.

Storage options

1. Choose *Define Fields* from the File menu, or press ⇧⌘-**D**. The Define Fields dialog box appears.
2. Create the field you want to use with Auto Enter, following steps 2 through 4 in "Adding fields" on page 49.
3. Once you have created the Field name and field type, click the Options button. The Entry Options dialog box appears.
4. Click the Storage Options button. The Storage Options dialog box appears.
5. Select the radio button describing the type of storage options you want to use.
6. Click the OK button in the Storage Options dialog box.
7. Click the OK button in the Entry Options dialog box.
8. Click the Done button in the Define Fields dialog box.

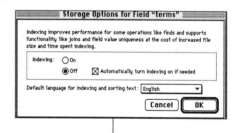

Storage options manage indexing capabilities, which are associated with relational database capabilities. The default entry is Off, with the checkbox labeled Automatically turn indexing on if needed selected.

For more information on storage options and relational databases, see Chapter 14, "Relational concepts," on page 149.

Additional Auto Enter options

The Validation option checks to make sure when data is entered that:

▲ *The data is either a number, date, or time.*

▲ *The field is not empty, is unique, or that data exists for that field.*

▲ *The data is part of a value list. For more information on value lists, see "Value lists" on page 57.*

▲ *The data falls within a defined number range.*

▲ *The data cross-checks with another calculated value. For more information on calculated values, see "Creating basic calculations" on page 108.*

▲ *The data is not being overwritten by another entry (Strict).*

▲ *A customized message appears if the data fails the validation test.*

■ Validation

The pop-up menu at the top of the Entry Options dialog box lets you choose to either automatically enter data or validate.

To use data validation:

1. Choose *Define Fields* from the File menu, or press ⇧⌘-**D**. The Define Fields dialog box appears.

2. Create the field you want to use with Auto Enter, following steps 2 through 4 in "Adding fields" on page 49.

3. Once you have created the field name and field type, click the Options button. The Entry Options dialog box appears.

4. Choose *Validation* from the pop-up menu. The Validation dialog box appears.

5. In the Validation dialog box, select the options you wish to use.

6. Click the OK button in the Entry Options dialog box.

7. Click the Done button in the Define Fields dialog box.

You can validate information in any of three FileMaker Pro 3 types: Number, Date, or Time.

Not empty makes sure something is in this field. Unique looks for something different, such as a social security number. Existing makes sure something is existing in the field.

You can specify that whatever is entered be an option listed on an existing value list.

This option lets you specify a range of numbers for validation.

You can specify a calculation that cross-checks results.

Choose this option to prevent the user from typing anything in the field.

This option causes a custom message you type in the box below to appear when anything that is entered is considered not valid.

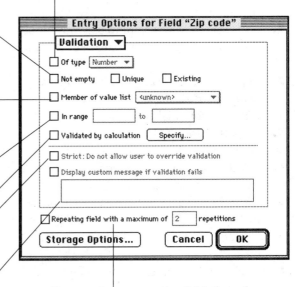

You can also set repeating fields from the Validation view of the Entry Options dialog box.

■ Value lists

Value lists are lists of choices that are attached to a field. When the user enters data in this field, the choices can be presented as a pop-up menu, checkbox list, or radio button list.

To create a value list:

1. Choose *Define Fields* from the File menu, or press ⇧⌘-**D**. The Define Fields dialog box appears.

2. Create the field you want to use with a value list, following steps 2 through 4 in "Adding fields" on page 49.

3. Once you have created the field name and field type, click the Options button. The Entry Options dialog box appears.

4. Choose *Validation* in the pop-up menu at the top of the dialog box. The Validation panel appears.

5. Select the Member of value list checkbox.

6. Choose *Define Value Lists* from the Member of value list pop-up menu. The Define Value Lists dialog box appears.

7. In the Value List Name box, type a name for the value list.

8. Click the Create button. The Value List Name now appears in the scrolling list at the top of the dialog box.

9. In the custom values scrolling box, type a list of the values you wish to have available for this field. Be sure to press the Return key after each value.

10. Click the Done button in the Define Value Lists dialog box.

11. Click the OK button in the Entry Options dialog box.

12. Click the Done button in the Define Fields dialog box.

13. In the Layout mode, proceed to "Formatting value lists" on page 60 to complete the process.

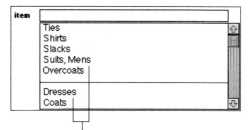

This is a sample value list shown in the pop-up list format. The user can click on a choice, instead of having to enter the information by typing.

This list has an additional feature. It is a divided list, with a ruler line appearing between categories of information.

Here is the Member of value list pop-up menu. The last entry, Define Value Lists, is how you create a new list.

If you have never defined a value list before, this entry reads <No Lists Defined>.

This scrolling list shows value lists that have already been created.

Here is where you type the name of the value list.

└ Here is where you type the items you wish to have in your value list.

Creating sections in a divided value list

A value list can be divided into logical sections, in the same way the layouts menu can be divided, by placing a straight line between portions of the list.

To divide a value list:

1. Choose *Define Fields* from the File menu, or press ⇧⌘-**D**. The Define Fields dialog box appears.
2. Select the Member of value list checkbox.
3. Choose *Define Value Lists* from the Member of value list pop-up menu. The Define Value Lists dialog box appears.
4. Select the value list you wish to change from the Define Value Lists scrolling box.
5. In the custom values scrolling list, press the Return key at the end of a value where you want the division to appear.
6. On a line by itself, type a hyphen (-). Press the Return key again if you need to move a value down one line.

7. Click the Done button in the Define Value Lists dialog box.
8. Click the OK button in the Entry Options dialog box.
9. Click the Done button in the Define Fields dialog box.

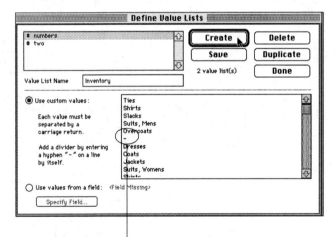

Type the hyphen between the divisions, making sure that the hyphen appears on its own line. See "Value lists" on page 57 for an example of a value list in a layout.

Duplicating a value list

You might want to duplicate a list if you want to use a similar list of items. Once you have created a duplicate list, you can then edit the items, adding, changing, or deleting any items on the list.

To duplicate a value list:

1. Using steps 1 through 4 on page 58, select the value list you wish to duplicate from the Define Value Lists scrolling box.
2. Click the Duplicate button. The new value list appears in the Define Value Lists scrolling box. This list has the same name as the list it was created from, with the word Copy appearing at the end of the name.
3. To change the name, in the Value List Name box, type a new name for this newly created list. The old name disappears.
4. Click the Save button.
5. Click the Done button in the Define Value Lists dialog box.

The scrolling list from the Define Value lists dialog box

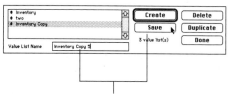

Notice the name has the word Copy appearing after it. You can change the name, but don't forget to click the Save button.

Deleting a value list

1. Using steps 1 through 4 on page 58, select the value list you wish to delete from the Define Value Lists scrolling box.
2. Click the Delete button. The Delete dialog box appears.
3. Click the Delete button in the Delete dialog box if you want to make the deletion;
   or
   Click the Cancel button if you change your mind and do not want to make the deletion.
4. Click the Done button in the Define Value Lists dialog box.

One of the nicest things about FileMaker Pro 3 is that it often gives you some kind of warning when you are about to make a mistake.

Here's another warning box you'll see when you try to delete a value list.

Value lists

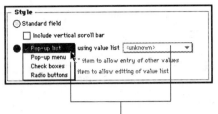

This is the pop-up menu where you choose the format for your value list. Notice the value list pop-up menu just to the right.

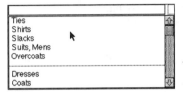

This is a pop-up list. This type of field format has scroll bars.

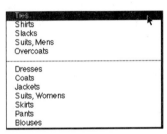

This is the pop-up menu. This type of list has no scroll bars and shows the entire list.

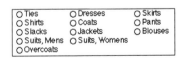

You can select more than one checkbox at a time.

However, you can select only one radio button at a time on a list.

The Behavior panel at the bottom of the Field Format dialog box contains two important options you might want to use.

■ Formatting value lists

1. In the Layout mode, select the field containing a value list that you want to format.

2. Choose *Field Format* from the Format menu, or press ⌘-**F**.

3. Select the radio button with the pop-up menu.

4. From the pop-up menu, select the format you want the field to have. Your choices are:
▲ Pop-up list
▲ Pop-up menu
▲ Checkboxes
▲ Radio buttons

5. From the value list pop-up menu, select the associated value list to use.

6. If you want to allow other items that are not on the value list to be entered into the field, select the Include "Other" checkbox that appears just below the value list pop-up menu. The designation "Other" appears on the list.

7. If you want to allow items on the value list to be edited, select the Include "Edit" checkbox that appears just below the value list pop-up menu.

8. If you want other items to be entered into the field, select the Allow entry into field checkbox from the Behavior panel.

9. If you want the entire contents of the field to be selected on entry, select the Select entire contents checkbox.

10. Click the OK button.

Behavior
☒ Allow entry into field
☐ Select entire contents of field on entry

■ Standard fields

Sometimes you type more information in a field than fits in the on-screen field size. To see the contents of a normal field that contains more information than fits on screen, you need to add scroll bars.

To add scroll bars:

1. In the Layout mode, select the field you want to add scroll bars to.
2. Select *Field Format* from the Format menu. The Field Format dialog box appears.
3. At the top of the Field Format dialog box, select the Standard field radio button.
4. Select the Include vertical scroll bar checkbox just below the Standard field radio button.
5. Click the OK button.

Both the Standard field radio button and the checkbox below need to be selected to create scroll bars on a standard field.

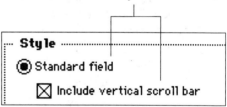

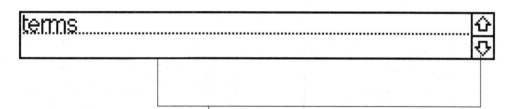

Here is how the field looks once scroll bars have been added. You can reshape the field and make it as deep as you like. This field allows two lines of data entry before you must use the scroll bars to see the rest of the text.

■ Container fields

Container fields can contain pictures. This is the field type you need to use if you want to create a database of pictures.

To create a container field:

1. In the Layout mode, choose *Define Fields* from the File menu, or press ⇧⌘-**D**. The Define Fields dialog box appears.
2. Type a field name in the Field Name box.
3. Select the Container radio button, or press ⌘-**O**.
4. Click the Create button.
5. Click the Done button.
6. Drag the field into position on the layout.

Entering data into a container field

These fields are considerably different from regular data entry fields. You must import your picture into the field instead of typing anything into the field. For more information on importing pictures and movies, see "Adding pictures" on page 105.

To import a picture into the field:

1. In the Browse mode, click inside of the container field.
2. Choose *Import Picture* or *Import Movie* from the Import/Export submenu in the File menu. The Please select a file dialog box appears.
3. From the scrolling list in the dialog box, select the picture you wish to import.
4. Click the Open button.

Creating a container field is no different from creating a text field. What is different is how you enter information. You must use the Import Picture or Import Movie choice from the Import/Export submenu in the File menu.

Container fields

■ Global fields

Global fields are handy fields for entering one piece of data that you use often and that doesn't change. Some examples include a logo, a company name and address, or a person's name. Global fields are a shortcut way of placing information into a layout.

To create a global field:

1. In the Layout mode, choose *Define Fields* from the File menu, or press ⇧⌘-**D**. The Define Fields dialog box appears.
2. Type a field name in the Field Name box.
3. Select the Global radio button, or press ⌘-**G**. The Options for Global Field dialog box appears.
4. Select the type of information you wish the global field to hold from the Data type pop-up menu. The choices include:
   ▲ Text
   ▲ Number
   ▲ Date
   ▲ Time
   ▲ Container
5. Click the OK button.
6. Click the Done button.
7. Drag the field into position on the layout.

Using a global field

1. In the Browse mode, enter the information into the global field that you wish to be uniform across records.
2. Select a new record. The global field is filled in with the global information.

Global fields need one more step—you must fill out the options. You can use any field type, and a global field could even be a repeating field.

■ Sample layout

Expense Summary layout

To create a report just like this one, you will have to refer to other sections of the book. These sections are clearly noted by the layout illustrated below. To see the finished product, refer to the next page.

The information on who submitted the report is created by selecting *Current User Name* from the *Paste Special* submenu in the *Edit* menu. The "submitted by" field label is typed text.

See "Paste Special commands" on page 44 to learn about special commands. See "Adding new text to the layout" on page 95 to learn how to type field labels and other text in a layout.

The Expense Summary for box is created by using the text tool, filling the background with black, and typing the text in white. A hairline was drawn in black from the left-hand side of the page to the right, lining up exactly under the text box.

See "Text Color" on page 72 for how to create the black-and-white box. See "Adding lines" on page 94 for how to create a hairline.

The parts used in this layout include:

▲ Title Header, with the submitted by and report title information

▲ Body, with company information and record number used as an ID number

▲ Sub-summary by Company (trailing), with two summary fields

▲ Footer, with date pasted in using Paste Special

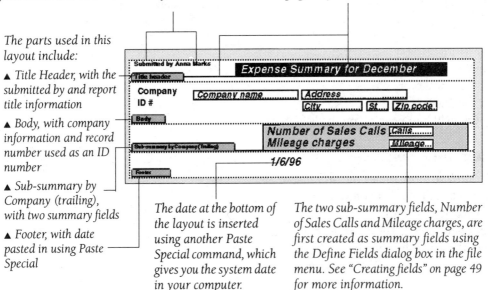

The date at the bottom of the layout is inserted using another Paste Special command, which gives you the system date in your computer.

The two sub-summary fields, Number of Sales Calls and Mileage charges, are first created as summary fields using the Define Fields dialog box in the file menu. See "Creating fields" on page 49 for more information.

Finished Expense Summary layout

This report is a quick way to find out any kind of categorized information that needs subtotals. The first category is the person who submitted the report, followed by each company as a category in itself. The last things you see after the company information are the two fields that add up entries for each company: Number of Sales Calls and Mileage charges.

As the entry screen for this report is used, each salesperson enters the sales call numbers for the day and the costs.

When the report is submitted, the database is sorted out by salesperson and company. This last step is what makes the report actually work. Until the sorts are done, the summary figures won't show up on screen or in a printout.

```
Submitted by: Anna Marx     Expense Summary for December

Company     Digital Press
   ID # 1                          Oakland        CA

                           Number of Sales Calls   6
                                Mileage charges  $2.00

Company     ReMarx Fibres          792 Stow Ave.
   ID # 2                          Oakland     CA    94606

                           Number of Sales Calls   4
                                Mileage charges  $3.15

Company     Jengi's Farm           793 Old Mill Road
   ID # 3                          Sedona      AZ

                           Number of Sales Calls   2
                                Mileage charges  $13.20

Company     Quinella Superior      R.R. 3, Box 45
   ID # 4                          Klamath Falls  OR

                           Number of Sales Calls   3
                                Mileage charges  $17.30
```

Formatting text & fields

5

■ Format menu

The Format menu contains options for changing text appearance and text, number, date, time, or graphics formats. These formats make information appear in a certain way, such as making the date print out as 11/30/96.

There are two additional choices, Field Format and Field Borders, which determine how lists of data are displayed and whether a field is outlined with a border or not.

Selecting fields and labels

Before you apply text formats, you must know how to choose a field, a label, or individual characters or words within a label.

▲ To choose a field or an entire label, in the Layout mode use the pointer tool to click in the middle of the field or label.

Selecting part of a label

1. To select a character or two, or a word from a label in the Layout mode, select the text tool from the toolbox then select the label, or double-click the label using the pointer tool.
2. Drag the pointer over the characters or word you wish to select.

When a label or field is selected, small square dots appear at each corner. These dots are called handles.

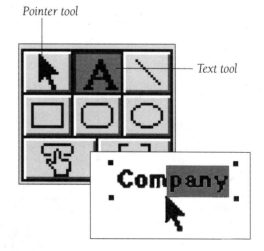

Pointer tool

Text tool

✔ **Note:** *Sometimes when you apply text attributes to a label, the label text appears to be on two or more rows. If that happens you must expand the label area.*

———Select this handle.

Drag to the right to make the label box longer. Drag down to make the box deeper. Once the box is large enough, you can see all of the text.

✔ **Tip:** *You can choose more than one field and apply text attributes by holding down the Shift key while you are selecting the fields. Once you have selected all of the fields you want to change, let go of the Shift key and choose the text attributes.*

Expanding labels or fields

1. To expand a label or field, in the Layout mode, use the pointer tool from the toolbox to select the label or the field.

2. Drag on the lower right-hand corner of the label area handle. To expand the box to the right, drag right; to expand the box down, drag down.

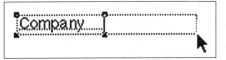

This is an example of a field being enlarged. You can see the original end of the field, where the handles appear, and the new size, indicated by the dotted lines that extend out to the right.

■ Formatting the font

1. In the Layout mode, select the field(s) or label(s) you want to change.

2. Choose *Font* from the Format menu. The Font submenu appears.

3. Select the font you want to use.

4. If the font you want to use has a small triangle indicating a submenu, choose the font from the submenu. Your field now appears in the new font.

This selected font, AGaramond, has a submenu with six versions of AGaramond on it.

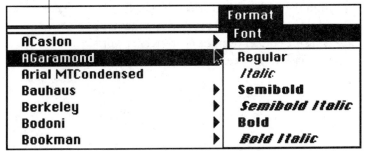

Size

1. In the Layout mode, select the field(s) or label(s) you want to change.
2. Choose *Size* from the Format menu. The Size submenu appears.
3. Choose the size you want to use.
4. If the size does not appear, choose Custom at the bottom of the Size menu. The Custom font size dialog box appears.
5. Type the size you want to use in the Custom font size box.
6. Click the OK button.

6 Point
8 Point
9 Point
10 Point
✓ 12 Point
14 Point
18 Point
24 Point
36 Point
48 Point
72 Point
Custom...
16 Point

The selected size has a check mark beside it. Additional sizes can be created using the Custom command on the bottom of the Size menu.

✔ **Tip:** *Font sizes must be in whole numbers. FileMaker Pro 3 does not support fractional sizes of fonts such as 12.5 points.*

This is where you type the font size.

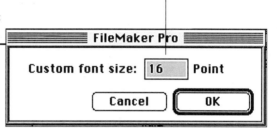

Style

1. In the Layout mode, select the field(s) or label(s) you want to change.
2. Choose *Style* from the Format menu. The Style submenu appears.
3. Choose the style you want to use.

✔ **Tip:** *Remember AGaramond on the previous page? That font had a submenu listing a Bold version of AGaramond. If you use a font that is listed as a bold font on the font menu, you do not need to select Bold from the Style menu.*

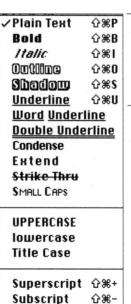

The major styles have shortcut keys for quicker access.

Left-aligned text

Left-aligned text is lined up on the left-hand side.

Center-aligned text

*Centered text is centered
in either
the label area or the field.*

Right-aligned text

*Right-aligned text is lined up
on the right-hand side.*

Full-aligned text

Full-aligned text is lined up evenly on both the left and right sides. This option is often used for newsletters.

■ Align text

1. In the Layout mode, select the field(s) or label(s) you want to change.
2. Choose *Align* from the Format menu. The Align submenu appears.
3. Choose the alignment you want to use. You have four choices:
   ▲ Left, or ⌘-[
   ▲ Center, or ⌘-\
   ▲ Right, or ⌘-]
   ▲ Full, or ⇧⌘-\
4. To change the position of the text within the field box, choose one of the three choices:
   ▲ Top, which aligns the text at the top of the field box
   ▲ Center, which places the text in the vertical center of the field box
   ▲ Bottom, which places the text at the bottom of the field box

The Line Spacing command on the Format menu gives you single or double spacing.

The Custom command shows the Paragraph dialog box, which gives you a greater range of choices for paragraph spacing and indentations.

■ Line Spacing

The Line Spacing command lets you change single spacing to double spacing, and also gives you access to the Paragraph dialog box where you can change the alignment, the indentions, and the spacing above and below a paragraph.

To change the line spacing:

1. In the Layout mode, select the field(s) or label(s) you want to change.
2. Choose *Line Spacing* from the Format menu. The Line Spacing submenu appears.
3. Choose either Double or Single.

Line Spacing Paragraph dialog box

1. In the Layout mode, select the field(s) or label(s) you want to change.

2. Choose *Line Spacing* from the Format menu. The Line Spacing submenu appears.

3. Choose Custom from the Line Spacing submenu. The Paragraph dialog box appears.

4. Change the alignment, indentions, and line spacing.

5. Click the Tabs button to set tabs (see "Setting tabs" on page 73 for more explanation).

6. Click the OK button.

These alignment buttons are yet another way of changing text alignment.

Line Spacing Height works like double spacing. Type how many empty lines you want to have between the lines of type in this box.

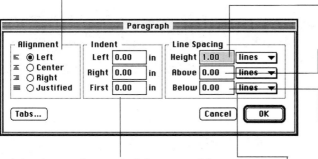

Line Spacing Above gives you extra space above the paragraph. Type how many blank lines you want to appear before the paragraph starts.

Line Spacing Below gives you extra space below the paragraph. Type how many blank lines you want to appear after the paragraph ends.

A left indention changes the left margin of the paragraph, like this:

> *Carolyn requested far too many bags of popcorn for the circus to sell.*

Right indention changes the right margin, and first indention changes how much just the first line of the paragraph is indented—like an initial tab.

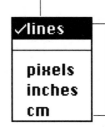

The pop-up lists on the right of the Line Spacing measurement boxes let you change the way of measuring distance between and within the paragraph.

Line Spacing

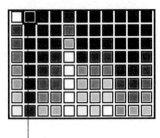

Drag the pointer over the Text Color palette until you come to a color you want to use, then let go.

Text Color

1. In the Layout mode, select the field(s) or label(s) you want to change.
2. Choose *Text Color* from the Format menu. The Text Color palette appears.
3. Choose the color you want the text to be from the Text Color palette.

The text ruler stays up on top of the screen in either the Browse or the Layout modes, and gives you quicker access to many formatting features associated with text.

Font pop-up menu   Size pop-up menu   Bold, italic, and underline   Indention buttons   Tab buttons   Measurement pop-up menu

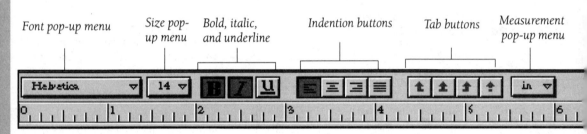

✔ **Tip:** *To see the text ruler in the Browse mode, find it on the Format menu. In the Browse mode, the text ruler will show you the margins of a field when you select that field.*

■ Using the text ruler

1. In the Layout mode, select the field(s) or label(s) you want to change.
2. Choose *Text Ruler* from the Show menu.
3. To change the font, choose the font pop-up menu, then choose the font you want to use.
4. To change the font size, choose the size pop-up menu, then choose the size you want to use.
5. To use one of the enhancements, bold, italic, or underline, choose the appropriate button.
6. To change the text alignment using the text tool from the tools panel, click anywhere inside of the text, then choose the appropriate button. To use the text ruler to set tabs, see page 73.

■ Setting tabs

Before setting tabs, you must turn on the text ruler so you can see where you might want the tabs to appear.

Selecting the text ruler and tabs

1. In the Layout mode, choose *Text Ruler* from the Show menu. The text ruler appears.
2. Select the fields you want to change.
3. Choose *Custom* from the Line Spacing submenu in the Format menu, then click the Tabs button.
4. Select the radio button for the type of tab alignment you want.
5. Type the position for the tab in the Position box. Look at the ruler for a visual check.
6. If you want dot leaders or any other character to fill the line, type the character you want to use in the Fill Character box.
7. Click the New button for the first tab. Use the New button whenever you wish to add another tab and the Set button for changes.
8. Click the OK button.

Changing tabs

1. Complete steps 1 through 3 in "Selecting the text ruler and tabs" above.
2. To change a tab, select the tab from the scrolling list, then type a new position for the tab in the Position box.
3. Click the Set button.
4. Click the OK button.

Deleting tabs

1. Complete steps 1 through 3 in "Selecting the text ruler and tabs" above.
2. To delete a tab, select the tab from the scrolling list.
3. Click the Clear button.
4. Click the OK button.

✔ **Tip:** *You can set tabs for one record by accessing the text ruler while you are in the Browse mode. Choose Text Ruler from the Format menu, click on the proper tab button, then click where you want the tab to appear.*

Left, center, right, and Align On tab alignment buttons

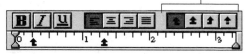

Text ruler with tabs

Tab Type radio buttons

Position box

Here is where you type in a fill character.

Setting tabs

■ Formatting data types

When you enter text, numbers, dates, or times, you can choose how they appear, regardless of how they were entered.

Formatting text fields

The Text command on the Format menu controls the font, size, color, style, and paragraph options for field and label text.

There they are again—fonts, sizes, colors, and styles. The Style panel in this dialog box contains more styles than are available from the text ruler.

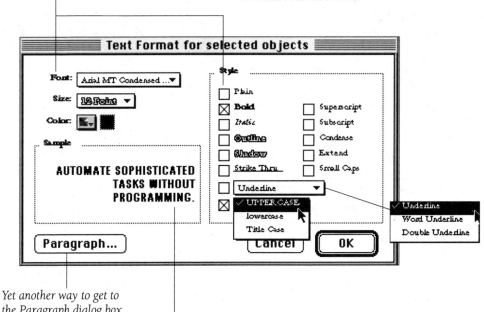

Yet another way to get to the Paragraph dialog box.

You can see a preview of how your text will appear in the Sample box.

To use the formatting options for Text fields:

1. In the Layout mode, select the field(s) or label(s) you want to change.
2. Choose *Text* from the Format menu. The Text Format dialog box appears.
3. Make any changes you wish using the Font, Size, and Color pop-up menus.
4. Choose any option in the Style panel.
5. To change the paragraph options, click the Paragraph button. See "Line Spacing Paragraph dialog box" on page 71 for more details about the Paragraph dialog box.
6. Click the OK button.

■ Formatting number fields

1. In the Layout mode, select the field(s) you want to change. Make sure the field is designated as Number type in the Define Fields dialog box. See "Adding fields" on page 49 for information on the Define Fields dialog box.

2. Choose *Number* from the Format menu. The Number Format dialog box appears.

3. Make any changes you need in the Number Format dialog box. See the next sections for details on various panels in that dialog box. Watch your changes in the Sample box, which shows you how the new format affects any text.

4. Click the OK button.

The Number Format dialog box has five major sections: Leave data formatted as entered, Format as Boolean, Format as decimal number, Separators, and Negative number formats.

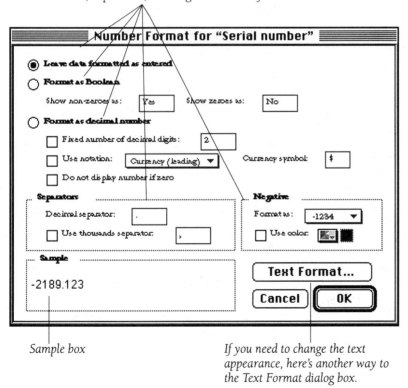

Sample box

If you need to change the text appearance, here's another way to the Text Format dialog box.

Boolean formatting is handier than you'd think. You can enter a number one way and have FileMaker Pro 3 show you an answer.

Boolean formatting

The Number Format dialog box will let you display one text message if a field contains zero and another text message if the amount is other than zero. The preset message is "No" for zero amounts and "Yes" for any entry greater than zero.

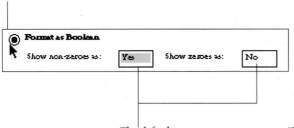

The default messages are set up as "Yes" and "No." Type a new message in the boxes if you want something else to be displayed.

When you click in the field you see what was entered.

Dues paid [13.20]

Dues paid [Yes]

When you click in any other field, you see the result of the Boolean formatting.

✔ **Idea:** *Practical uses of Boolean formatting—If you want to see if club members have paid their dues, regardless of the amount they have paid, make the amount field a Boolean field.*

When you enter the amount the member paid, the program displays "Yes" or, if you change the message in the Number Format dialog box, "Paid."

Later when you are looking for unpaid members, the task will be easy.

To use Boolean formatting in a field:

1. In the Layout mode, select the field(s) you want to change.
2. Choose *Number* from the Format menu. The Number Format dialog box appears.
3. In the Number Format dialog box, choose the Format as Boolean radio button.
4. In the Show non-zeros as box, the default message "Yes" is displayed. If you have a number greater than zero entered in this field, the field displays "Yes." If you want to display another message, enter the word or words you wish to have displayed here.
5. In the Show zeros as box, the default message "No" is displayed. If you have entered either zero or a blank in this field, the field displays "No." If you want to display another message, enter the word or words you wish to have displayed here.
6. Click the OK button.

Formatting number fields

Decimal number formats

1. In the Layout mode, select the field(s) you want to change.
2. Choose *Number* from the Format menu. The Number Format dialog box appears.
3. In the Number Format dialog box, choose the Format as decimal number radio button.
4. Select any of the options you wish to use.
5. Click the OK button.

Be as precise as you need to be. Type the number of decimal places you want here (the default is 2).

If you're trading in yen, or prefer pounds sterling, you can change the currency symbol by inserting the proper character in this box.

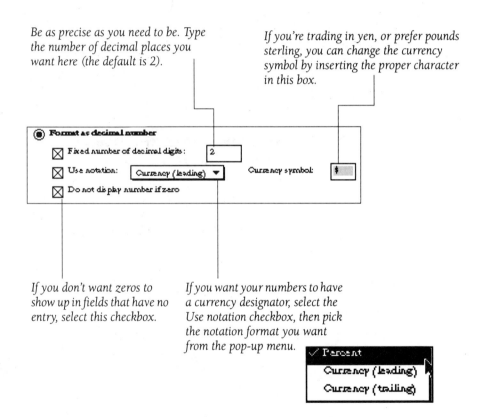

If you don't want zeros to show up in fields that have no entry, select this checkbox.

If you want your numbers to have a currency designator, select the Use notation checkbox, then pick the notation format you want from the pop-up menu.

The Format as pop-up menu gives you five choices for the format. In addition, you can change the default color of red to any color that is on the color palette.

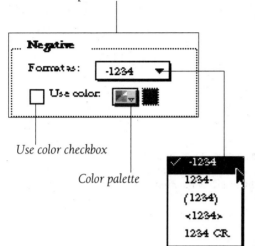

Use color checkbox

Color palette

Negative numbers

1. In the Layout mode, select the field(s) you want to change.
2. Choose *Number* from the Format menu. The Number Format dialog box appears.
3. Select the Format as decimal number radio button and choose the options you wish to use.
4. Choose the negative number format you want to use from the Format as pop-up menu in the Negative panel.
5. If you wish your negative number to appear in color, select the Use color checkbox. The default color is red.
6. To change the default color, choose the color panel palette and select the color you want to use from the palette.
7. Click the OK button.

Text Format from the Number Format dialog box

You can access the Text Format dialog box by clicking the Text Format button in the Number Format dialog box. For more information on text formats, see "Formatting text fields" on page 74.

■ Formatting date fields

1. In the Layout mode, select the field(s) you wish to format.
2. Choose *Date* from the Format menu. The Date Format dialog box appears.
3. Select the Format as radio button.
4. Select the format you wish to use from the Format as pop-up menu. Watch your changes in the Sample box, which shows you how the new format affects any text.
5. Click the OK button.

✔ **Tip:** *Make sure the field is designated Date format in the Define Fields dialog box. See "Adding fields" on page 49 for information on the date fields and the Define Fields dialog box.*

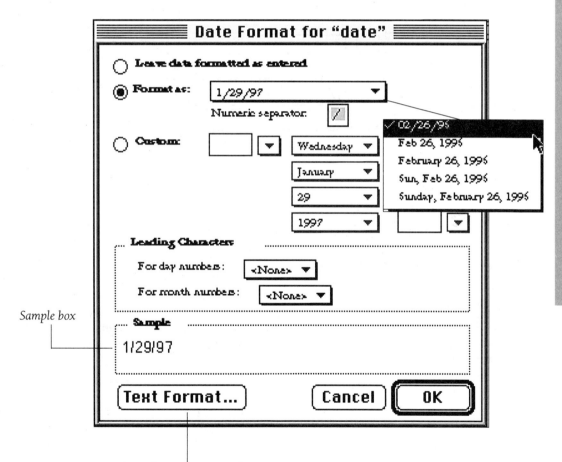

Sample box

Here's another way to get to the Text Format menu.

Formatting date fields

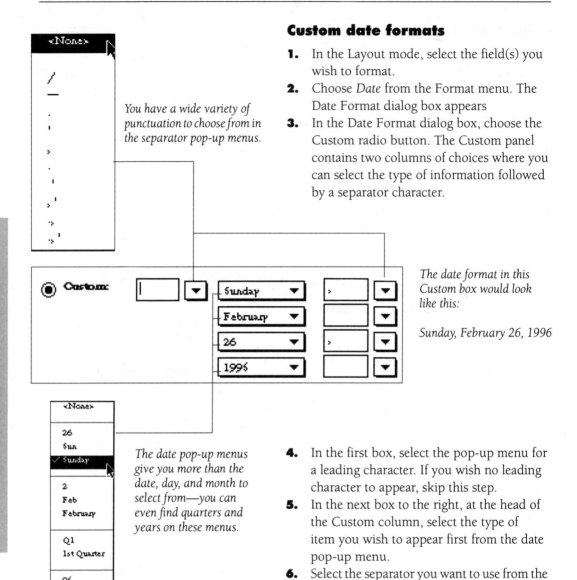

Custom date formats

1. In the Layout mode, select the field(s) you wish to format.
2. Choose *Date* from the Format menu. The Date Format dialog box appears
3. In the Date Format dialog box, choose the Custom radio button. The Custom panel contains two columns of choices where you can select the type of information followed by a separator character.

You have a wide variety of punctuation to choose from in the separator pop-up menus.

The date format in this Custom box would look like this:

Sunday, February 26, 1996

The date pop-up menus give you more than the date, day, and month to select from—you can even find quarters and years on these menus.

4. In the first box, select the pop-up menu for a leading character. If you wish no leading character to appear, skip this step.
5. In the next box to the right, at the head of the Custom column, select the type of item you wish to appear first from the date pop-up menu.
6. Select the separator you want to use from the separator pop-up menu at the right of the first date format pop-up menu. Continue selecting formats and separators, using the next set of three boxes.
7. Click the OK button.

Formatting date fields

Leading characters

If your date is in numeric format, for example, 12/3/98, you can decide whether or not you want leading zeros for the month and date.

To set the leading characters:

1. In the Layout mode, select the field(s) you wish to format.

2. Choose *Date* from the Format menu. The Date Format dialog box appears.

3. Select the Format as radio button from the Date Format dialog box.

4. Select the first format from the Format as pop-up menu.

Start by selecting the top menu choice from the Date Format dialog box.

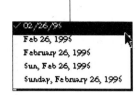

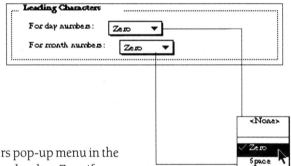

5. On the For day numbers pop-up menu in the Leading Characters panel, select Zero if you want your days to have a preceding zero, for example, 1/09/97; select Space if you want your date to have a preceding space.

6. On the For month numbers pop-up menu in the Leading Characters panel, select the leading character (either Space or Zero) you want to use for the month.

7. Click the OK button.

✔ **Tip:** *Make sure the field is designated Time format in the Define Fields dialog box. See "Adding fields" on page 49 for information on the date fields and the Define Fields dialog box.*

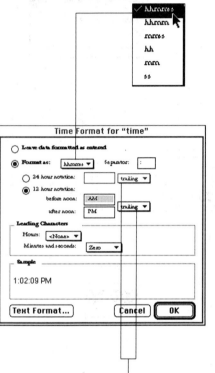

Both the 24 hour notation and 12 hour notation radio buttons have additional formatting choices you can make.

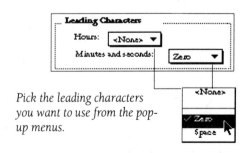

Pick the leading characters you want to use from the pop-up menus.

■ Formatting time fields

1. In the Layout mode, select the field(s) you wish to format.
2. Choose *Time* from the Format menu. The Time Format dialog box appears.
3. In the Time Format dialog box, select the Format as radio button.
4. Choose the time format you wish to use from the Format as pop-up menu.
5. Type in the separator character in the Separator box. The default choice is a colon.
6. Click the OK button.

12 or 24 hour notation

1. In the Layout mode, select the field(s) you wish to format.
2. Choose *Time* from the Format menu. The Time Format dialog box appears.
3. In the Time Format dialog box, decide if you wish your time to be displayed in 12 hour or 24 hour notation.
4. To have a special character to appear before or after the 12 or 24 hour time, type that character in the box following your choice.
5. Select trailing or leading from the pop-up menu following your choice.
6. Click the OK button.

Leading characters

1. In the Layout mode, select the field(s) you wish to format.
2. Choose *Time* from the Format menu. The Time Format dialog box appears.
3. In the Leading Characters panel of the Time Format dialog box, select leading zeros or spaces from the Hours pop-up menu for the hour numbers.
4. Select leading zeros or spaces from the Minutes and seconds pop-up menu for the minutes and seconds numbers.
5. Click the OK button.

■ Sample layout

Enhancing the Recipe layout
from Chapter 3

In Chapter 3 we introduced a recipe template that can be made more efficient by changing a few field definitions. Here's what we suggest:

▲ Type of recipe field contains a major category such as Main dishes. Change this field type to a pop-up list so you won't have recipe types that are all slightly different.

▲ Category of recipe field is the same type of exercise as Type of recipe. Make it a pop-up list and the data entry will be faster and easier.

▲ Ingredients fields could be a repeating field with a dozen or so repetitions.

These two fields are excellent candidates for pop-up lists. Pop-up lists help keep data entry consistent.

The Marks' Family Cookbook

Main dishes

Poultry

Recipe Name Chicken a la Charlotte   Serves 4

Ingredients

4 large double chicken breasts, boned
1 cup cream
1/2 cup flour
2 Tbsp Nutmeg
Salt and pepper to taste
2 packages frozen artichoke hearts
2 large onions, thinly sliced

3 cups cooked rice, in a casserole dish

Instructions

Saute artichoke hearts and onions in butter until the onions are just barely limp. Set aside.
Place the flour, nutmeg, salt, and pepper in a plastic bag, and shake the chicken breasts inside of the bag to cover with flour.
Brown the chicken breasts in the left over butter from the onions.
Place browned chicken over the rice in the casserole, then the vegetables, add cream and more nutmeg.

Cooking temperature 350
Cooking time 1 1/4 hours
Source of recipe unknown

Notes cook as slow as possible, can add a little cooking sherry to improve flavor.

Advanced formatting

■ Size and page margins

To see the page margins:

▲ In the Layout mode, choose *Page Margins* from the Show menu. The margins of the layout will appear.

Since there are no real left, right, top, or bottom margins assigned in FileMaker Pro 3, the placement of the fields and text determines how close they are to the edge of the paper. You can use the Size command to see how large the part is.

Seeing and changing the part size

1. In the Layout mode, choose *Size* from the Show menu. The Size window appears.

2. Select any part label to see the size in the Size window.

3. Click in one of the direction boxes and type a new measurement.

4. Press the Tab key to move to the next measurement box.

5. Click the close box in the Size window.

Changing units of measurement

1. In the Layout mode, choose *Set Rulers* from the Mode menu.

2. Select the units of measurement you want to use from the Units pop-up menu.

3. Click the OK button.

Part label

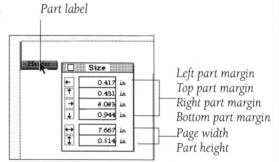

Left part margin
Top part margin
Right part margin
Bottom part margin
Page width
Part height

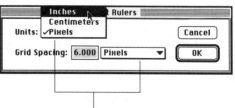

There are two pop-up menus in the Set Rulers dialog box. One sets the unit of measurement (Inches, Centimeters, or Pixels), the other sets the grid spacing to help you line up objects and text.

✔ **Tip**: *The AutoGrid command from the Arrange menu, or ⌘-Y turns the ruler increments into "magnets" that attract any object you place. This is known as a Snap To command in some other programs. Turn AutoGrid on to help you line up objects as you place them.*

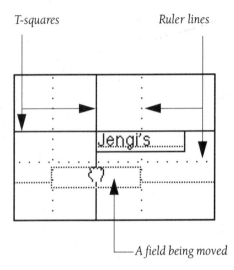

T-squares   Ruler lines

— *A field being moved*

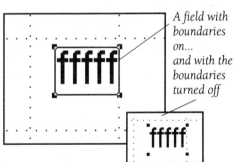

A field with boundaries on...
and with the boundaries turned off

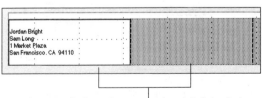

This sample data shows a mailing label (with the ruler lines turned on). Notice the blank space to the right where the next label will appear.

■ Tools to help line up text

Ruler lines

Ruler lines are basic grid lines that do not print, but appear in the Layout mode to help you line up text and objects. To turn on the ruler lines:

▲ In the Layout mode, choose *Ruler Lines* from the Show menu. The ruler lines appear as faint dotted lines in the layout.

T-squares

T-squares help you line up objects even more flexibly than ruler lines. You can move the T-square lines around:

1. In the Layout mode, choose *T-Squares* from the Show menu, or press ⌘-T.

2. Drag either the horizontal or vertical T-square line into position and move the text or fields up against it.

Text boundaries

Normally when you type text in the layout, such as a field label or a header, the text appears surrounded by four dots—one on each corner. You can turn on a solid boundary, making it easier to see the text:

▲ In the Layout mode, choose *Text Boundaries* from the Show menu. A solid line will appear around any selected text instead of just four corner handles.

Sample data

It's easier to see if your layout is correct if you can imagine the actual information in it. You don't need to switch back and forth between the Browse mode and the Layout mode to do this. To show sample data in your layout:

▲ In the Layout mode, choose *Sample Data* from the Show menu. The current record's information will appear in the layout.

■ Field borders

Although you can enter data without clearly
seeing the boundaries of the field (the first click
approximately where the field is shows you the
boundaries), you may prefer to set up actual lines
that appear on any or all sides of the field.

To add borders:

1. In the Layout mode, select the field you want
to add borders to.
2. Choose *Field Borders* from the Format menu,
or press Option-⌘-**B**. The Field Borders
dialog box appears.
3. Select the checkboxes that describe where
you want the borders to appear.
4. Click the OK button.

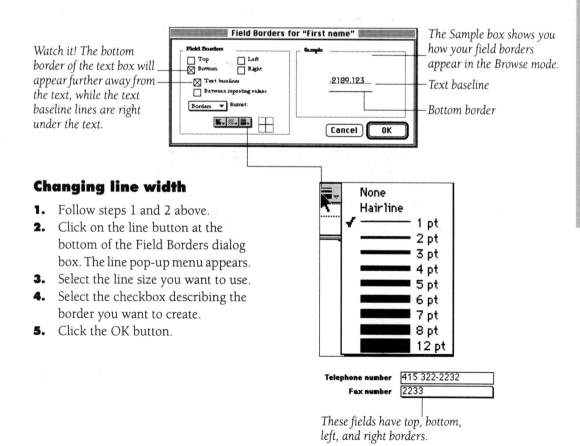

*Watch it! The bottom
border of the text box will
appear further away from
the text, while the text
baseline lines are right
under the text.*

*The Sample box shows you
how your field borders
appear in the Browse mode.*

Text baseline

Bottom border

Changing line width

1. Follow steps 1 and 2 above.
2. Click on the line button at the
bottom of the Field Borders dialog
box. The line pop-up menu appears.
3. Select the line size you want to use.
4. Select the checkbox describing the
border you want to create.
5. Click the OK button.

*These fields have top, bottom,
left, and right borders.*

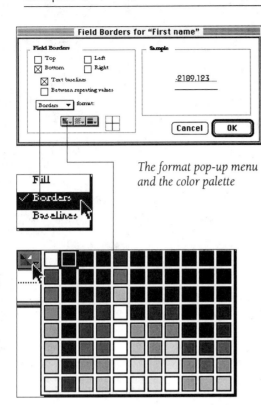

The format pop-up menu and the color palette

Adding color

You can add color to the borders and text baseline or fill the field with color.

To add color:

1. In the Layout mode, select the field you want to format.
2. Choose *Field Borders* from the Format menu, or press Option-⌘-**B**. The Field Borders dialog box appears.
3. Select the area you want to add color to from the format pop-up menu.
   ▲ Borders
   ▲ Fill
   ▲ Baseline
4. Click the color button. The color palette appears.
5. Select the color you wish to use.
6. To color other areas, repeat steps 3 through 5.
7. Click the OK button.

Removing color

To remove color, perform steps 1 through 4 above, and select the white color in the color palette.

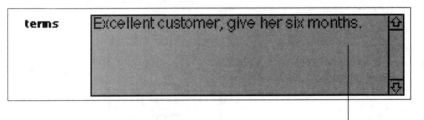

This scrolling text field is filled with light green.

✔ **Idea:** *Color code your work. Entering information is easier to do if areas on your layout are different colors. For example, use blue for basic information, green for financial information, gold for prospective sales or customers.*

Field borders

Adding patterns

It's hard to read the text if you have a patterned background, so be sure to make the background color light, the text bold, and the pattern not too busy. You can add patterns to lines or fills.

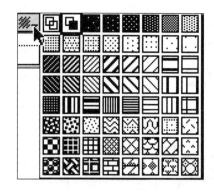

To add a pattern:

1. In the Layout mode, select the field you want to format.
2. Choose *Field Borders* from the Format menu, or press Option-⌘-**B**. The Field Borders dialog box appears.
3. Select the area you want to add a pattern to from the format pop-up menu.
4. Click the pattern button. The pattern palette appears.
5. Select the pattern you wish to use.
6. To add a pattern to other areas, repeat steps 3 through 5.
7. Click the OK button.

✔ **Tip:** *Pick a pattern that won't be too distracting, then color it in a light color. Go back into the Layout mode and use the text ruler to make the text bold.*

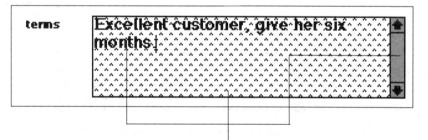

This is the same field as on page 88, using different colors, including a colored border with a background. Notice the text is now bold.

Removing patterns

Patterns are removed using the pattern palette. These two buttons are the first buttons on the pattern screen. The button on the left stands for no pattern and no color. The button on the right stands for solid color and no pattern. Select the button you want to use to remove the pattern.

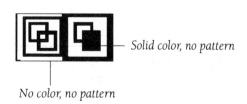

Solid color, no pattern

No color, no pattern

Field borders

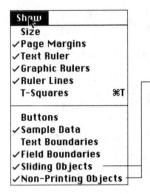

Sliding and non-printing objects can be seen in the Layout view if you select them on the Show menu. They will show up with a heavy, gray outline around the field.

■ Sliding fields

Sliding fields enable you to move an empty field up or to the left in order to fill in the gap.

To use sliding fields:

1. In the Layout mode, select the field you want to apply sliding fields to.

2. Choose *Sliding/Printing* from the Format menu, or press Option-⌘-T.

3. Select a sliding checkbox, either Sliding left or Sliding up.

4. Click the OK button.

Sliding left moves any empty fields to the left. You might want to use this when you have an arrangement like this:

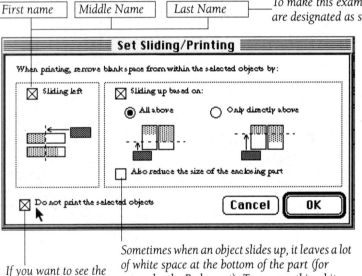

To make this example work, all three fields are designated as sliding objects.

Sliding up—You have two choices, to move all fields up, or to move just one field up.

You might use this when you have fields arranged like this:

| Name |
| Company |
| Address |
| City, State, Zip |

If you want to see the field on the screen, but do not want it to print, select this checkbox.

Sometimes when an object slides up, it leaves a lot of white space at the bottom of the part (for example, the Body part). To remove this white space, select this checkbox.

Nonprinting text and objects

The Set Sliding/Printing dialog box also controls whether or not a field will print, even though it shows on the screen.

To not print a field, select the Do not print the selected objects checkbox on the Set Sliding/Printing dialog box.

✔ **Tip:** *You can reuse the same alignment choices by choosing Align from the Arrange menu, or pressing ⌘-K.*

■ Using alignment

Alignment is a more automatic way of making fields, text, and objects, such as a drawn box, line up in the layout.

To set an object's alignment:

1. In the Layout mode, select all of the fields, text, or objects you want to line up.

2. Choose *Set Alignment* from the Arrange menu, or press ⇧⌘-κ.

3. Select the correct radio button in the Top to Bottom or Left to Right panels. Watch the sample boxes. It's easy to accidentally pile everything up in one stack.

4. Click the OK button.

Arrange	
Group	⌘G
Ungroup	⇧⌘G
Lock	⌘H
Unlock	⇧⌘H
Bring to Front	⇧⌥⌘F
Bring Forward	⇧⌘F
Send to Back	⇧⌥⌘J
Send Backward	⇧⌘J
Align	⌘K
Set Alignment...	⇧⌘K
AutoGrid	⌘Y

Here are the Top to Bottom radio buttons. The last button, Distribute space, is handy for creating equal spacing between fields.

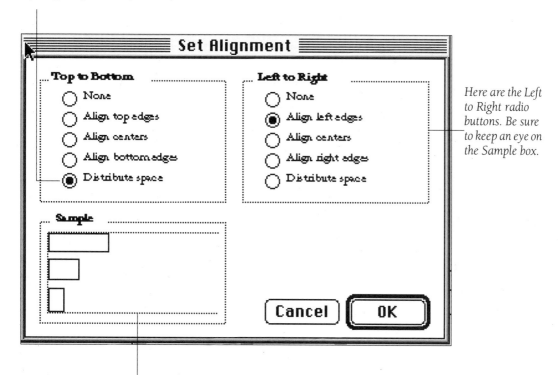

Here are the Left to Right radio buttons. Be sure to keep an eye on the Sample box.

Never, never forget to check the Sample box.

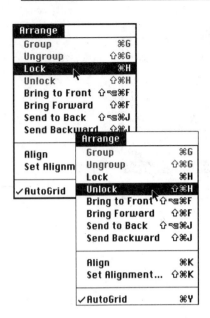

■ Locking fields, text, and objects

Locking fields prevents anyone from moving the fields while in the Layout mode. Unlocking is the reverse of locking—you are turning the lock off so the fields can be moved.

Locking fields

1. In the Layout mode, select the field(s), text, or objects you wish to lock.
2. Choose *Lock* from the Arrange menu, or press ⌘-H. The fields are locked now.

Unlocking fields

1. In the Layout mode, select the field(s), text, or objects you wish to unlock.
2. Choose *Unlock* from the Arrange menu, or press ⇧⌘-H.

■ Sample layout

Sliding fields are absolutely wonderful. They close up the gaps, fill in the blanks, and make a cumbersome layout sing. If you're an old FileMaker Pro 2 user, you'll remember sliding fields were used in labels. No longer—check out the section "Labels" on page 31 for the new way of creating mailing labels.

✔ **Tip:** *Sliding fields work with individual fields and will not work with repeating fields, which are basically multiple instances of the same field.*

Sliding field example

Here is a telephone directory layout that uses sliding fields to advantage. The actual layout is simple—it's the sliding fields that make it work.

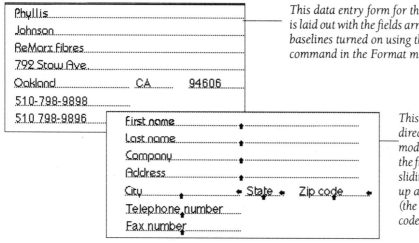

This data entry form for the telephone directory is laid out with the fields arranged down the page, baselines turned on using the Format Borders command in the Format menu.

This is the telephone directory in the Layout mode. Notice that all of the fields are designated as sliding fields, both sliding up and sliding sideways (the City, State, and Zip code fields).

These two entries from the telephone directory illustrate how sliding fields appear when you are using the Preview mode.

The first entry, for Emily Mars, slides the City, State, and Zip code together so there are no gaps—a much more professional look.

Jengi's Farm has almost no information. The Address is missing and so are the telephone numbers and the Zip code, but the entry remains nice and compact on the screen and the printout.

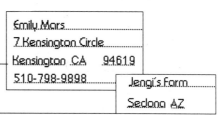

Adding text & graphics

■ Adding new text to the layout

Field labels

Some text is added automatically when you create a field—the field label is added by default. When you drag the Field button over from the toolbox, a field label as well as a new field is added.

To prevent a field label from being added, remove the check mark from the Create field label checkbox in the Specify Field dialog box.

Adding regular text

1. In the Layout mode, select the text tool from the toolbox.
2. Choose *Text Ruler* from the Show menu.
3. Select the font, font size, enhancements, and alignment you wish to use from the text ruler.
4. Click in the layout where you wish the text to appear.
5. Type the text.
6. When you are finished typing, click outside of the text area.

Moving the text

1. Select the pointer tool from the toolbox.
2. Drag the text box to the proper position.

Make sure this checkbox is blank if you don't want a field label to be created.

Use the "A," called the text tool, to create text.

Use the pointer tool to move text and objects.

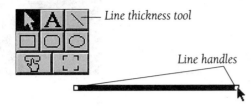

Line thickness tool

Line handles

■ Adding lines

FileMaker Pro 3's graphics consist of simple lines, rectangles, rounded rectangles, or circles. You can use these basic shapes to enhance layouts.

Using the line tool

1. In the Layout mode, select the line tool from the toolbox.
2. Click the line thickness button in the toolbox.
3. Select the line thickness from the line thickness pop-up menu.
4. Click where you want the line to start and drag the pointer to the end of the line.

Keeping the line straight

To keep the line straight vertically or horizontally, hold the Shift key down while you are dragging the pointer.

Shortening or lengthening the line

Once the line is drawn, you see handles on the ends of the line. To shorten or lengthen the line:

1. In the Layout mode, select the line.
2. Position the pointer over the handle on the end of the line you want to shorten or lengthen.
3. Drag the line to the new length.

Changing the line thickness

1. In the Layout mode, select the line.
2. Click the line thickness button in the toolbox.
3. Select the new line thickness from the line thickness pop-up menu.

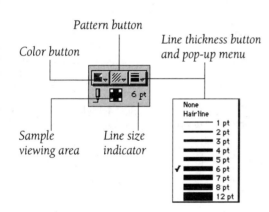

Pattern button

Color button

Line thickness button and pop-up menu

Sample viewing area

Line size indicator

■ Adding color and pattern

Coloring the line

1. In the Layout mode, select the line.
2. Click the color button in the toolbox.
3. Select the color from the color palette.

Adding a pattern to the line

1. In the Layout mode, select the line.
2. Click the pattern button in the toolbox.
3. Select the pattern from the pattern palette.

*The color and pattern palettes work
exactly the same way.*

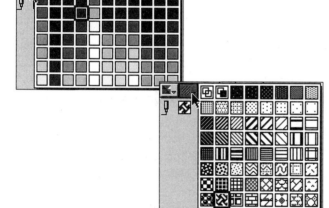

Priddy's Products

This line has been filled with both a
pattern and color.

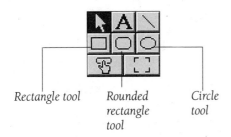

Rectangle tool   *Rounded*   *Circle*
               rectangle   *tool*
               tool

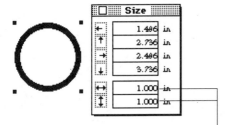

You can change measurements of an object using the Size window. Enter the measurements you want to change in these two size boxes.

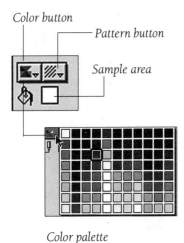

Color palette

■ Drawing

Drawing can be used to create backgrounds for text, or to create other objects by stacking various shapes together.

Drawing simple shapes

1. In the Layout mode, select one of the object drawing tools, either the rectangle, rounded rectangle, or circle tools.
2. Click in the layout where you want one side of the object to start.
3. Drag the pointer to the left to make the object wider, or down to make the object longer.

Drawing round circles and perfect squares

1. In the Layout mode, select one of the object drawing tools, either the rectangle, rounded rectangle, or circle tools.
2. Hold the Shift key down and drag the pointer until the object is drawn.

Checking the object size

1. In the Layout mode, select one of the objects you have drawn.
2. Choose *Size* from the Show menu. The Size window appears. Refer to the chart at the left to see the size.

Adding filled color

1. In the Layout mode, follow steps 1 through 3 in "Drawing simple shapes" above to draw the rectangle, rounded rectangle, or circle.
2. Click the color button in the toolbox. The color palette appears.
3. Select the color you wish to use from the color palette. The object is filled with that color.

Adding filled patterns

1. In the Layout mode, follow steps 1 through 3 in "Drawing simple shapes" on page 98 to draw a rectangle, rounded rectangle, or circle.
2. Click the pattern button in the toolbox. The pattern palette appears.
3. Select the pattern you wish to use from the pattern palette. The object appears filled with that pattern.

Changing the surrounding line of the object

When you draw an object, the line that draws the object is taken from the line thickness button. To change a line thickness, see "Adding lines" on page 96.

Removing color and pattern from lines and objects

1. In the Layout mode, select the object or line you wish to change.
2. Click the color button for either lines or objects, depending on what it is you are trying to change. The color palette appears.
3. Select the white color in the color palette.
4. Click the pattern button for either lines or objects, depending on what it is you are trying to change. The pattern palette appears.
5. Select the empty button.

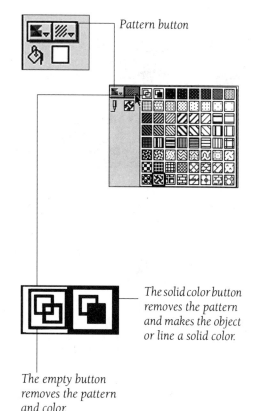

Pattern button

The solid color button removes the pattern and makes the object or line a solid color.

The empty button removes the pattern and color.

Drawing

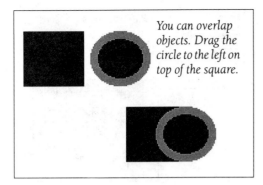

You can overlap objects. Drag the circle to the left on top of the square.

This drawing contains one rounded rectangle, one circle, and one square.

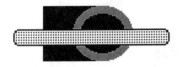

Here we selected the long rounded rectangle and chose Send Backward. It's now behind the circle, but on top of the square.

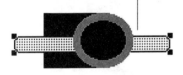

This time we selected the long rounded rectangle and chose Send to Back, to the bottom of the stack.

■ Drawing a complex object

You can overlap, or stack, objects together to make a second object. When you do this the objects are still individual parts.

Simple multiobject drawing

1. In the Layout mode, select an object drawing tool—rectangle, rounded rectangle, or circle—from the toolbox.
2. Draw at least two objects.
3. Drag one object on top of another object.

Move backward or forward

1. In the Layout mode, select one of the objects that is in the stack.
2. Choose one of the four following commands from the Arrange menu to move that object relative to all of the other objects in the stack.
   ▲ *Bring to Front*, or Option-⇧⌘-**F**, which moves the selected object all the way to the top of the stack.
   ▲ *Bring Forward*, or ⇧⌘-**F**, which moves the selected object on top of the adjacent object.
   ▲ *Send to Back*, or Option-⇧⌘-**J**, which moves the selected object all the way to the bottom of the stack.
   ▲ *Send Backward*, or ⇧⌘-**J**, which moves the selected object back of the adjacent object.

Drawing a complex object

■ Combining text and graphics

This exercise shows you how to create the type of text you see in this invoice example.

We'll create this graphics and text bar exactly the way it is done in this invoice example.

Priddy's Products
Best Products for the Knitter in you

Invoice

Invoice for   Invoice Number

Date 3/15/93

Jordan Bright
Sam   Long   Terms Excellent customer
1 Market Plaza
OAKLAND   CA   94110

Item	Quantity	Price	Extension
Merilee's Wool/Alpaca Blend	392	12.15	$4762.80
		Total due	**$21887.73**

Priddy's
Best Products for the Kn
Invoice for

✔ Tip: *The graphic rulers show you vertical and horizontal measures.*

Creating a fancy text bar—Method 1

1. In the Layout mode, choose *Graphic Rulers* from the Show menu.
2. Select the text tool from the toolbox.
3. Type the text.
4. Click the fill color button and select black from the color palette. The rectangle is now filled with solid black.
5. Choose *Text Color* from the Format menu. The color palette appears.
6. Select white from the color palette.

This method gives a black background with white text, and the text is aligned in the box according to the *Align Text* command in the Format menu. If you want a special position for the text, or a wider text box, Method 2 might work better.

Select the rectangle, rounded rectangle, or circle tool from the toolbox to begin drawing a background shape.

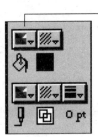

Use the color button in the tools palette to fill the shape. You could also fill the shape using the pattern button.

✔ **Tip:** *When you move an object, make sure the pointer is in the middle of the object. In this case, make sure the pointer is in the middle of the text, centered between all four handles.*

In this example, the circle is filled both with a color and a pattern, and white text is placed over the simple graphic.

Creating a fancy text bar—Method 2

1. In the Layout mode, choose *Graphic Rulers* from the Show menu.
2. Select the rectangle tool and draw a rectangle one and one-half inches long and one-quarter inch high.
3. Use the graphic rulers to measure as you draw, or adjust the size in the size dialog box, as shown on page 98.
4. Click the fill color button and select black from the color palette. The rectangle is now filled with solid black.
5. Choose *Text Ruler* from the Show menu.
6. Still in the Layout mode, and in an area away from the rectangle, select the text tool from the toolbox.
7. Select the font and size for the text from the text ruler. This sample used Helvetica 12 point.
8. Type the text.
9. Choose *Text Color* from the Format menu. The Text Color palette appears.
10. Select white (or any other highly contrasting color) from the Text Color palette. Remember where you typed that text.
11. Select the pointer tool from the toolbox.
12. Click where you typed the text until you see the text box handles.
13. Drag the text box on top of the solid black rectangle, rounded rectangle, or circle.

Combining text and graphics

■ Grouping objects

When you move two objects so that one is on top of another, you still have two objects. You can group multiple objects into one object:

1. In the Layout mode, select all of the objects you wish to group together. You can select more than one object by holding down the Shift key while clicking on each object.
2. Choose *Group* from the Arrange menu, or press ⌘-**G**.

Arrange	
Group	⌘G
Ungroup	⇧⌘G
Lock	⌘H
Unlock	⇧⌘H
Bring to Front	⇧⌥⌘F
Bring Forward	⇧⌘F
Send to Back	⇧⌥⌘J
Send Backward	⇧⌘J
Align	⌘K
Set Alignment...	⇧⌘K
✓AutoGrid	⌘Y

Make sure you hold down all of the keys carefully in these four-key commands.

Ungrouping

Sometimes you need to break the objects apart to make a simple change. To do this, you must Ungroup the objects:

1. To ungroup an object, in the Layout mode select the object.
2. Choose *Ungroup* from the Arrange menu, or press ⇧⌘-**G**.

Select all of the objects, and make sure you see enough handles for every object.

Then choose Group and you have just one object.

You can group text boxes along with graphics objects.

✔ **Tip:** *Select All, or* ⌘-**A** *on the Edit menu will select everything on the layout.*

Grouping objects

Common commands

What you want to do	Command and keys
Eliminate text within a field, fields, objects, lines, or pictures that you might want to use somewhere else	Cut ⌘-x
Duplicate text of any kind, field information, fields, objects, lines, or pictures	Copy ⌘-c
Use the copy you just made	Paste ⌘-v
Eliminate text within a field, fields, objects, lines, or pictures	Clear Delete key

✔ **Tip:** *The Clear key on the keyboard does not delete an object. Use the Delete key instead.*

✔ **Important:** *You must use Undo immediately, before you perform any other operation.*

■ Copying objects

You can copy text boxes, lines, objects, or pictures in much the same way you would in your word processing program.

Copying objects within the database

You can copy from one layout to another, or copy and paste within the same layout.

To copy an object:

1. In the Layout mode, select the object(s) you wish to copy.
2. Choose *Copy* from the Edit menu, or press ⌘-c.
3. Click where you want the copy to go.
4. Choose *Paste* from the Edit menu, or press ⌘-v.

You can
   ▲ Paste into the same layout
   ▲ Switch layouts before pasting
   ▲ Switch databases before pasting

■ Deleting objects

1. In the Layout mode, select the object(s) you wish to delete.
2. Choose *Clear* from the Edit menu;
   or
   Choose *Cut* from the Edit menu (or press ⌘-x) if you might want to paste the object later.

Undoing changes

Immediately choose *Undo* from the Edit menu, or press ⌘-z, if you need to undo whatever it was that you just did.

■ Adding pictures

FileMaker Pro 3 contains translators that help import pictures into your layouts.

To add a picture from an outside source:

1. In the Layout mode, choose *Import Picture* from the Import/Export submenu in the File menu. The Please select a file dialog box appears.

2. Choose the appropriate file format from the Show pop-up menu.

3. Choose the file from the file scrolling list.

4. Click the Open button. The picture appears in the layout.

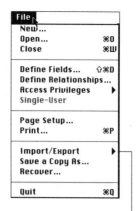

Select the picture location here.

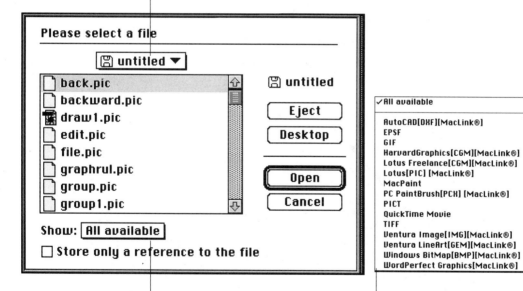

✔ **Tip:** *Slick trick—Select the Store only a reference to the file checkbox to keep the file size down. That way when FileMaker Pro 3 needs to show the picture, it will look the picture up on your hard disk, instead of placing a copy of the picture in the database permanently.*

Select the file type from the Show menu here.

Adding pictures

Calculated fields

■ Before we begin

You can perform calculations with the information
in your database using FileMaker Pro 3's Calculation field type. You can multiply fields together,
multiply fields by a number, or even add text
together. There are two types of *calculated fields*:
fields that perform basic calculations and fields
that perform summary calculations.

Specify Calculation dialog box

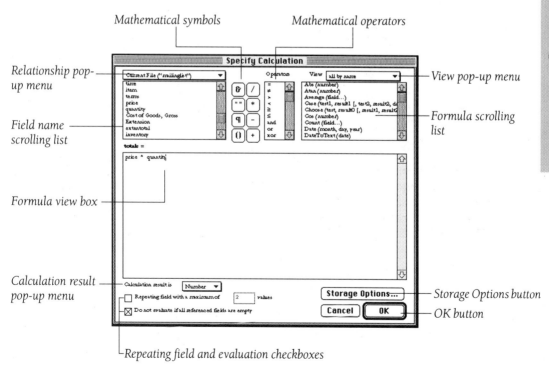

Mathematical symbols

Mathematical operators

Relationship pop-up menu

View pop-up menu

Field name scrolling list

Formula scrolling list

Formula view box

Calculation result pop-up menu

Storage Options button

OK button

Repeating field and evaluation checkboxes

Before we begin

■ Creating basic calculations

Before you begin, make sure you have two fields that are designated as Number type fields already created. *Calculations* are performed on Number type fields; *concatenations* are performed on Text type fields.

To create a basic calculation field:

1. In the Layout mode, choose *Define Fields* from the File menu, or press ⇧⌘-**D**. The Define Fields dialog box appears.
2. Enter a field name in the Field Name box.
3. Select the Calculation radio button in the Type panel, or press ⌘-**C**.
4. Click the Create button. The Specify Calculation dialog box appears.
5. Double-click the first field you want to use in your calculation from the field name scrolling list. The field appears in the formula view box.
6. Click on the mathematical symbol for the operation you intend to perform.
   - ▲ / stands for division
   - ▲ * stands for multiplication
   - ▲ - stands for subtraction
   - ▲ + stands for addition

You may also type these symbols using the keyboard.

7. Double-click on the second field you want to use in your calculation from the field name scrolling list.
8. Click the OK button in the Specify Calculation dialog box.
9. Click the Done button in the Define Fields dialog box.

Double-click items in the field name, operators, or functional formula lists to select them.

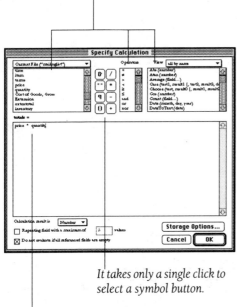

It takes only a single click to select a symbol button.

The formula appears here in the formula view box.

✔ **Tip:** *You can perform math on numeric fields, calculation fields, or a combination of those fields and numbers.*

Creating basic calculations

■ Editing a formula

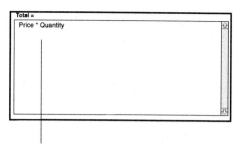

1. In the Layout mode, choose *Define Fields* from the File menu, or press ⇧⌘-**D**. The Define Fields dialog box appears.
2. In the field name scrolling list, select the field you want to change.
3. Click the Options button at the bottom of the Define Fields dialog box. The Specify Calculation dialog box appears.
4. Perform one of the actions from the chart below.
5. Click the OK button.
6. Click the Done button.

All editing takes place in the formula view box in the Specify Calculation dialog box. Notice the current field name just above the box—this reminds you which calculated field you are currently working on.

Formula editing

Desired action	How to do it
Add a field into the formula	**1.** Click where you want the field to appear. **2.** Double-click the field you want to add in the field scrolling list.
Delete a field from the formula	**1.** Double-click on the field in the formula. **2.** Press the Delete key, or select another field from the scrolling list.
Delete an entire formula	Press the Clear key.
Edit text added to the formula	**1.** Drag over the text until it is selected. **2.** Type the new text or press the Delete key to delete it.
Change mathematical symbols	**1.** Select the symbol you wish to change in the formula view box. **2.** Select a new symbol from the symbol buttons. You may also type the new symbol using the keyboard.
Change mathematical operators	**1.** Select the operator you wish to change in the formula view box. **2.** Select a new operator from the Operator scrolling list. You may also type the new operator using the keyboard.
Change functional formulas	**1.** Press the Clear key to delete the current formula. **2.** Select the correct functional formula from the functional formula scrolling list.

Editing a formula

Mathematical symbols

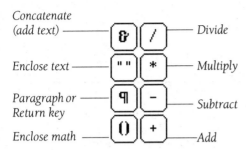

Concatenate (add text) ——— 𝕰

Enclose text ——— " "

Paragraph or Return key ——— ¶

Enclose math ——— ( )

——— / Divide

——— * Multiply

——— – Subtract

——— + Add

■ Mathematical symbols

Mathematical symbols are the glue that holds a formula together. The symbols determine the type of math and the order of operations. See "Creating basic calculations" and "Editing a formula" for information on using the mathematical symbols.

Mathematical symbols

Symbol	Meaning	Example
Concatenate &	Use concatenate to add two text fields together, or to add text that is not in a field to text that is in a field.	First name & " "& Last name "Ms. " & Last name City & ", " & State & " " & Zip
Enclose text " "	Enclose text is used to surround actual text that is to be concatenated.	"How are" & " " & "you"
Paragraph or Return key ¶	The paragraph symbol creates a new line at the point at which you insert it. This symbol works only in text, and not between fields.	"Credit balance¶Do not pay" gives the results: Credit balance Do not pay
Enclose math ( )	When math is performed, all multiplication and division operators are done first, then the addition and subtraction operations take place. Use the enclose math symbol as you would ordinary parentheses to make sure math is performed in a specific order. You may also type the parentheses into your formula using the keyboard.	Rate * (Overtime / Prorate - Base) *or* 34 * (3/2 - 25) **WARNING:** If you use the enclose math symbol or type in parentheses, you can create complicated formulas. That's OK, because the formulas will work—just be sure to count the number of parentheses to make sure you have matching pairs.
Divide /	Divide one field by another field	Hours / Days
Multiply *	Multiply two fields together	Rate * Hours
Subtract -	Subtract one field from another	Total hours - Regular hours
Add +	Add two fields together	Overtime pay + Regular pay

■ Mathematical operators

Operators give a formula the capability of comparing the contents of two or more fields.

You can make the comparison and get back a numerical result, or, if you specify that the result appear in Boolean format, you can see both the numerical result and either "Yes" or "No." See "Boolean formatting" on page 78.

The Operators scrolling list—Use this list just like the symbol buttons. To select an operator, double-click the operator. You can also type it using the keyboard.

Mathematical operators

Operator	Meaning	Example
=	Equal—Two or more items are equal	Total amount = Amount paid
≠	Not equal—Two or more items are not equal	Date ≠ Today
>	Greater than—One item is greater than the other	Raise > (Rate * .2)
<	Less than—One item is less than the other	Hours < 40
≥	Equal to or greater than—One item is equal to or greater than the other	Mortgage ≥ 150,000
≤	Equal to or less than—One item is equal to or less than the other	Earthquakes ≤ 1
and	And—Compares to see if two conditions exist	Mortgage ≥ 150,000 and Earthquakes ≤ 1
or	Or—Compares to see if one of two conditions exist	Earthquakes < 2 or Fires < 2
xor	Xor—Compares to see if one of two conditions does not exist (the opposite of or)	State = "CA" xor Name = "Sabatini" In other words, not anyone who is in California or who is named Sabatini—even if it's a Sabatini in Louisiana
not	Not—Compares to see if a condition is not met	State not "CA"
^	Exponentiation—Raises a number to a given power	Income ^ 2 Income to the power of two

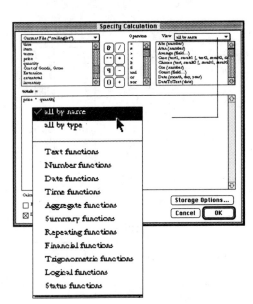

■ Functional formulas

Functional formulas have math built into the formula, so you don't have to work quite so hard. Functional formulas fall into several categories:

▲ Text functions   ▲ Repeating functions

▲ Number functions   ▲ Financial functions

▲ Date functions   ▲ Trigonometric functions

▲ Time functions   ▲ Logical functions

▲ Aggregate functions   ▲ Status functions

▲ Summary functions

View by type

1. In the Layout mode, choose *Define Fields* from the File manu, or press ⇧⌘-**D**. The Define Fields dialog box appears.

2. Enter a field name in the Field Name box.

3. Select the Calculation radio button from the Type panel, or press ⌘-**c**.

4. Click the Create button. The Specify Calculation dialog box appears.

5. Select the view you wish to use for the functional formulas from the View pop-up menu. You see only formulas of the selected type in the scrolling list.

6. Select the functional formula you wish to use from the scrolling list.

7. Click the OK button.

8. Click the Done button in the Define Fields dialog box.

■ Using a functional formula

Refer to Appendix A, "Functional formulas," on page 195 for samples and explanations of the most common functional formulas.

Using the IF formula

IF looks at a condition, decides if the condition is true, and then performs math or inserts text according to the condition.

The formula is IF(test, result one, result two). To use it:

1. Choose *Define Fields* from the File menu, or press ⇧⌘-**D**. The Define Fields dialog box appears.
2. Enter a field name in the Field Name box. (We used the field name Balance Status.)
3. Select the Calculation radio button, or press ⌘-**C**.
4. Click the Create button. The Specify Calculation dialog box appears.
5. Double-click the IF function in the function scrolling list. The sample IF function appears in the formula view box.
6. Double-click the formula area labeled *test*. In the formula area labeled test, substitute a condition you want the formula to examine. In our sample, we used *Grand total=Payment*.
7. Double-click the formula area labeled *result one*. For the result one area, enter what should happen if the condition is true. In our example, we entered the word "Paid."
8. Double-click the formula area labeled *result two*. For the result two area, enter what should happen if the condition is not true. In our example, we used the words "Past due."
9. Choose *Text* from the Calculation result pop-up menu. Otherwise you'll just see a 1 or 0.
10. Click the OK button.
11. Click the Done button in the Define Fields dialog box.

Three stages of the IF formula:

1. *The formula as it first appears*
2. *The formula with the condition in the test area*
3. *The final formula*

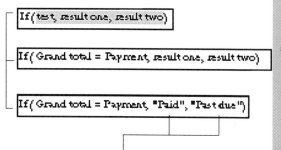

These results print out text, but you could have an IF formula that performs a calculation in the results area, too.

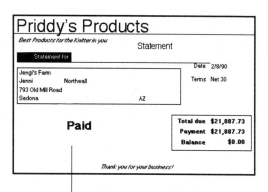

An elaborate IF formula that gives three results and examines two conditions.

If(Grand total = Payment, "Paid", If(Balance < 0, "Credit Balance -¶Do not pay", "Past due"))

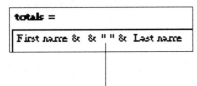

The First name and Last name fields are concatenated along with a blank space between the quotes so that the names will have a space between them and not appear as one long word:

> *Muriel Smart*
>
> *not*
>
> *MurielSmart*

■ Concatenating: Adding text

Adding text together is what we do when we form sentences. In FileMaker Pro 3, text can be added to other text or to fields.

1. In the Layout mode, choose *Define Fields* from the File menu, or press ⇧⌘-**D**. The Define Fields dialog box appears.
2. Enter a field name in the Field Name box.
3. Select the Calculation radio button, or press ⌘-**C**.
4. Click the Create button. The Specify Calculation dialog box appears.
5. Enter the text you wish to add in the formula view box according to one of the samples in the table below, and enclose the text in quotation marks.
6. Click the OK button.
7. Click the Done button in the Define Fields dialog box.

Concatenating text

Type of concatenation	Example
Text added to text	"Happy " & "Birthday " & "Mr. " & "President" (Notice the space that appears after the word but inside of the quotation marks.)
Text added to a field	"Honored " & Full name
Text fields added together	Full name & Title

The Golden rules of text concatenation

1. Text must be enclosed in quotation marks.

2. Type the text between the quotation marks exactly the way you want it to appear.

3. Use the & (ampersand) instead of the plus sign to add text and text fields.

4. Do not try to add text and numbers together.

5. Remember to add a space between words by adding a space between double quotes like this: "Mr." & " " & "President", or include the spaces between quotation marks with the words, as above ("Mr. ").

6. Use the paragraph symbol to insert a line break. Make sure you use this within the quotes such as: "Credit balance¶Do not pay".

■ Calculation results

How your results are displayed is a result of what you choose on the Calculation result pop-up menu. The default setting is Number, but if your results are supposed to print out text, you need to change this menu to display Text.

To use the Calculation result menu:

1. In the Layout mode, choose *Define Fields* from the File menu, or press ⇧⌘-**D**. The Define Fields dialog box appears.
2. Enter a field name in the Field Name box.
3. Select the Calculation radio button, or press ⌘-**c**.
4. Click the Create button. The Specify Calculation dialog box appears.
5. Enter the formula you want to use.
6. Select the proper calculation results from the Calculation result pop-up menu at the bottom of the Specify Calculation dialog box.
7. Click the OK button.
8. Click the Done button in the Define Fields dialog box.

✔ **Watch out!** *If FileMaker Pro 3 does not understand how to perform the calculation, perhaps because the wrong calculation results have been selected, you see a ? (question mark).*

✔ **Tip:** *When performing math on fields, make sure the fields are the same type (Number, Text, Date, or Time), and that the Calculation result menu matches the type of fields.*

What happens if...

Formula	Results in Browse mode	Calculation result menu choice
Price * quantity	$300.00	Number
IF(Balance=0,"Paid","Past due")	Paid or Past due	Text
Today + 30	January 12, 1996	Date
Time out - Time in	9:34	Time

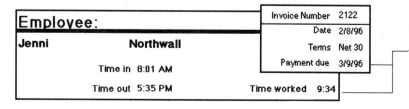

Sample time and date formulas—The Time formula subtracts the Time out from Time in; the Date formula adds 30 days to the invoice date.

The bottom of the Specify Calculation dialog box is where you will find the Calculation result menu (previous page) and two really useful checkboxes.

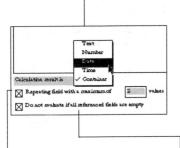

Here's another access to repeating fields. If your field is a calculation, this is where you set the number of repeats that are allowed.

The IF formula is an example of a formula that performs an evaluation. It checks to see if a field passes a test. If the field FileMaker Pro 3 is looking at contains no information, this checkbox prevents the calculation from taking place.

If(Grand total = Payment, "Paid", "Past due")

This part of the formula is the evaluation. If the Grand total field is blank, the formula will not continue if the Do not evaluate checkbox is selected.

■ Specify calculation checkboxes

There are two checkboxes at the bottom of the Specify Calculation dialog box. Each has a specific use that can be invaluable.

Repeating fields checkbox

If you have a calculation field, you cannot access the regular Options dialog box, which is normally the place to enter repeating fields. Options for calculated fields are calculations.

To set repeating fields:

1. In the Layout mode, choose *Define Fields* from the File menu, or press ⇧⌘-**D**. The Define Fields dialog box appears.
2. Enter a field name in the Field Name box.
3. Select the Calculation radio button, or press ⌘-**C**.
4. Click the Create button. The Specify Calculation dialog box appears.
5. Enter the formula you wish to use in the formula view area.
6. Select the Repeating fields checkbox and type in the maximum number of repeats you wish this field to have.
7. Click the OK button.
8. Click the Done button in the Define Fields dialog box.

Evaluation checkbox

Sometimes a formula requires FileMaker Pro 3 to look at a field and make a decision. An example is the IF formula on page 113. This is called a condition, test, or evaluation.

Selecting the Do not evaluate checkbox at the bottom of the Specify Calculation dialog box prevents the test from taking place if the field FileMaker is looking at has no information in it.

■ Summary fields

Summary fields summarize information. They give totals and grand totals for the fields in the entire database, or for any field you choose.

To create a summary field:

1. In the Layout mode, choose *Define Fields* from the File menu, or press ⇧⌘-**D**. The Define Fields dialog box appears.
2. Enter a field name in the Field Name box.
3. Select the Summary radio button, or press ⌘-**S**.
4. Click the Create button. The Options for Summary Field dialog box appears.
5. Select the radio button for the type of math you wish to have performed.
6. Select the field from the field name scrolling list that contains the information you wish to summarize.
7. If you need to exercise a more detailed option on the radio button, select the checkbox at the bottom of the field name scrolling list.
8. Click the OK button.
9. Click the Done button in the Define Fields dialog box.

Summary type radio buttons

Field name scrolling list

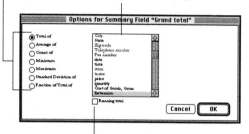

Detail checkbox—The contents of this checkbox depend on what type of math you have chosen from the radio buttons.

You can even perform simple statistics, such as standard deviations, using these radio buttons.

Summary fields

Summary fields

Using a summary field

Once you have created a summary field, it needs to be placed correctly in the layout in order to work. Summary fields require you to sort the database in a particular order. For information on sorting, see "Sorting" on page 121.

To set up a summary field in a layout:

1. In the Layout mode, drag the Part button over to the layout. The Part Definition dialog box appears.

If you want a summary to appear at the bottom of the layout, drag to the bottom of the layout. If you want it to appear at the top of the layout, drag to the top of the layout.

2. In the Part Definition dialog box, choose one of three part types:
▲ Leading Grand Summary, which always appears at the top of a report
▲ Sub-Summary when sorted by, which requires you to pick a sorting field from the field name scrolling list
▲ Trailing Grand Summary, which always appears at the bottom of a report

3. Select any other enhancements you want from the checkboxes at the bottom of the Part Definition dialog box, such as page break before or after.

4. Click the OK button.

5. Drag the summary field into the new summary part that appears in the layout.

This layout has four repeating fields in the Body part: Item, Quantity, Price, and Extension. Each field has six repetitions.

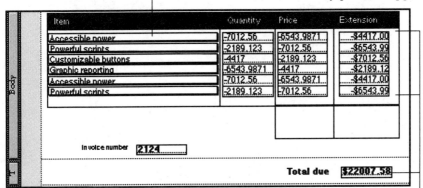

The Total due field is a summary field that adds up all of the Extension fields. It is placed in a Trailing Grand Summary part.

■ Relational formulas

Relational databases are databases that share information. They provide a way for one file to borrow information from another. You may use information in the related database just as you do information in your current database, for example, in mathematical calculations.

To borrow information, you must select the related file or define a relationship. For more information on relationality, see "Relational terms" on page 149.

To define a relationship:

1. In the Layout mode, choose *Define Fields* from the File menu, or press ⇧⌘-**D**. The Define Fields dialog box appears.
2. Enter a field name in the Field Name box.
3. Select the Calculation radio button, or press ⌘-**C**.
4. Click the Create button. The Specify Calculation dialog box appears.
5. Select the file that contains the field you want to use in your calculation from the relationship pop-up menu at the top of the Specify Calculation dialog box.
6. Double-click the first field you want to use in your calculation from the field name scrolling list. The field appears in the formula view box.
7. Click on the mathematical symbol for the operation you intend to perform.
8. Double-click on the second field you want to use in your calculation from the field name scrolling list.
9. Click the OK button in the Specify Calculation dialog box.
10. Click the Done button in the Define Fields dialog box.

When you want to use a field from a related database, select the file from the relationship pop-up menu.

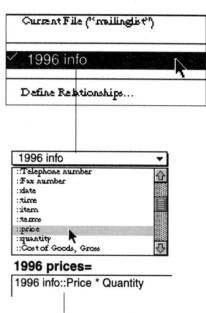

This formula multiplies the Price field from the related database, 1996 info, by the current file's Quantity field.

Notice the double colons between the related file name and the field name from that file.

■ Useful sample formulas

Finding how much time has passed

1. Create two fields, both designated as Time fields. Give one the name Time out and the other the name Time in.
2. In the formula view box, enter the following formula:

   Time out - Time in

3. Choose *Time* from the Calculation result pop-up menu.

Making multiple choices

1. Create a field you want to evaluate, for example, Balance due.
2. Create a calculation field to hold the formula, for example, balance status.
3. In the balance status formula view box, enter the following formula:

   IF(Balance due=0,"Paid",IF(Balance due<0, "Credit balance", "Past due"))

Explanation

1. First the database looks to see if the balance due is zero (Balance due=0). If that is true, it prints Paid in the balance status field.

   If that is not true, it proceeds to step 2.

2. If the balance is less than zero (Balance due<0), it prints Credit balance in the balance status field.

   If that is not true, it proceeds to step 3.

3. If the balance is not less than zero or not equal to zero (in other words, if someone still owes some money), it prints "Past due."

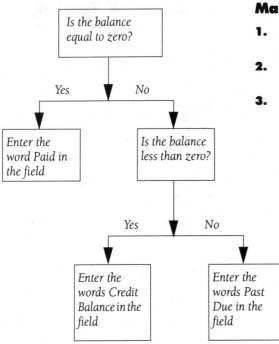

Just remember, you're a lot smarter than the computer—it can answer a question only yes or no. In other words, the computer can make only one of two decisions at a time, then it has to take another look.

Sorting & finding data

9

■ Sorting

Sorting is necessary to place records in a desired order; for example, placing a mailing list in zip code order or sorting in order to make a Sub-summary part work correctly.

Sorting entire database

1. Choose *Sort* from the Mode menu, or press ⌘**-s**. The Sort Records dialog box appears.
2. In the scrolling list of field names in the Sort Records dialog box, select the field you wish to sort by.
3. Click the Move button. The sorting field appears in the Sort Order scrolling list.
4. Select the order radio button from the bottom of the Sort Records dialog box.
Your choices include:
▲ Ascending order, or 0 to 9, and A to Z
▲ Descending order, or 9 to 0, and Z to A.
▲ Custom order
5. Click the Sort button.

✔ **Tip:** *Traditional sort order follows these rules:*
▲ *Numbers are sorted before letters.*
▲ *Uppercase letters are sorted before lowercase letters.*

Clear All, Move, Sort, Unsort, and Done buttons

Field name scrolling list

Sort Order scrolling list

Sort order radio buttons

Sort detail button

Sorting

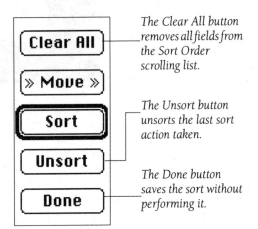

The Clear All button removes all fields from the Sort Order scrolling list.

The Unsort button unsorts the last sort action taken.

The Done button saves the sort without performing it.

Changing sort order

The previous sort order is retained in the Sort Records dialog box. The next time you sort, you see the sort order you just used.

To change the sort order:

1. Choose *Sort* from the Mode menu, or press ⌘-s. The Sort Records dialog box appears.
2. Click the Clear All button in the center of the Sort Records dialog box.
3. On the left-hand side of the Sort Records dialog box, select the new field you wish to sort by.
4. Click the Move button. The sorting field appears in the Sort Order scrolling list.
5. Select the order radio button from the bottom of the Sort Records dialog box.
6. Click the Sort button.

Saving the sort order

You can establish the sort order, then go back and perform the sort later.

To save a sort order:

1. Following steps 1 through 5 above, set up the sort the way you want it performed.
2. Click the Done button in the Sort Records dialog box.

Unsorting

1. Immediately after sorting, choose *Sort* from the Mode menu, or press ⌘-s. The Sort Records dialog box appears.
2. Click the Unsort button in the Sort Records dialog box.

✔ **Important:** *You must perform the unsorting procedure at right immediately after you sort, before you engage in any other operation.*

Sorting

■ Multiple sorts

Multiple sorts are performed when you need to sort information out by a category, then do a subsort within that category; for example, if you want to sort a mailing list by state then, within each state, by zip code.

To subsort information within a category:

1. Choose *Sort* from the Mode menu, or press ⌘-**s**. The Sort Records dialog box appears.
2. Click the Clear All button in the center of the Sort Records dialog box.
3. On the left-hand side of the Sort Records dialog box, select the new field you wish to sort by.
4. Click the Move button. The sorting field appears in the Sort Order scrolling list.
5. Select the field for the first subsort you want to perform and click the Move button.
6. Select the order radio button from the bottom of the Sort Records dialog box.
7. Click the Sort button.

How far do you want to go with this? You can create as many subsorts as you desire, but in practicality, unless your database is very, very large, one or two will do the job.

The sort is carried out in the order listed here in the Sort Order scrolling list. First the items are sorted by State, then within State by City, and last, within City by Zip code.

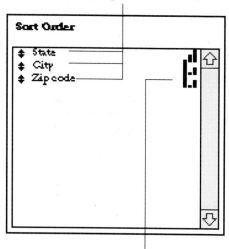

The symbols on the right-hand side of the Sort Order scrolling list tell you what type of sort is being performed: ascending, descending, or a custom sort.

Sample three-level sort	Sample three-level sort order
California	First sort (State)
Oakland	Second sort (City)
94601	Third sort (Zip code)
94602	
94606	
94611	
San Francisco	Second sort (City)
94111	Third sort (Zip code)
94114	
Oregon	First sort (State)
Portland	Second sort (City)
97201	Third sort (Zip code)
97204	
Tigard	Second sort (City)
97223	Third sort (Zip code)

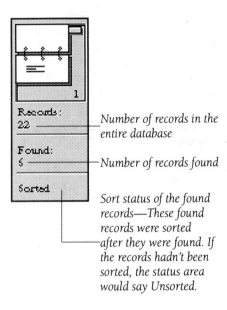

Records:
22 ———— *Number of records in the entire database*

Found:
5 ———— *Number of records found*

Sorted

———— *Sort status of the found records—These found records were sorted after they were found. If the records hadn't been sorted, the status area would say Unsorted.*

■ Sorting selected entries

Sorting selected entries means you have to first perform a find in order to select the entries.

To sort selected entries:

1. Perform a find to select the entries you want to sort. For information on finding entries, see "Finding records" on page 126.
2. Choose *Sort* from the Mode menu, or press ⌘-s. The Sort Records dialog box appears.
3. On the left-hand side of the Sort Records dialog box, select the field you wish to sort by.
4. Click the Move button. The sorting field appears in the Sort Order scrolling list.
5. Select the order radio button from the bottom of the Sort Records dialog box.
6. Click the Sort button when you are finished. Just the records you found will be sorted.

Sorting on summary fields

Normally, summary fields are excluded from the file name scrolling list in the Sort Order dialog box. They are easy to include, however:

▲ Select the Include summary fields checkbox at the bottom of the Sort Order scrolling list.

The field name scrolling list will not include any summary fields automatically. You need to select the Include summary fields checkbox.

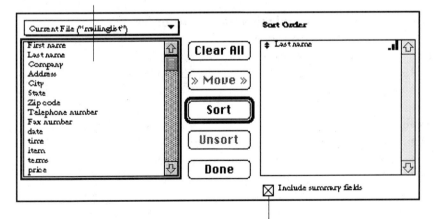

The Include summary fields checkbox

■ Sorting relational databases

Relational databases are databases that are linked in such a way that information can be shared. When a sort is performed, the database on the screen is sorted. The relational database, the database from which information is borrowed, is not sorted. You can sort relational databases without viewing them on the screen.

For more information on relationality, see "Relational terms" on page 149.

To sort a relational database while the main database is active:

1. Choose *Sort* from the Mode menu, or press ⌘-**s**. The Sort Records dialog box appears.

2. Choose the name of the relational file you wish to sort from the relationship pop-up menu at the top of the dialog box.

3. From the field name scrolling list in the Sort Records dialog box, select the field you wish to sort by. Notice these relational fields are preceded by two colons (::).

4. Click the Move button. The sorting field appears in the Sort Order scrolling list.

5. Select the order radio button from the bottom of the Sort Records dialog box.

6. Click the Sort button.

From the relationship pop-up menu at the top of the dialog box, you can sort your current file or a related file. If you have no related files, you also have an opportunity to define a related file.

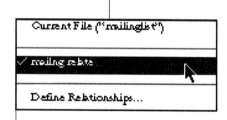

Relationship pop-up menu

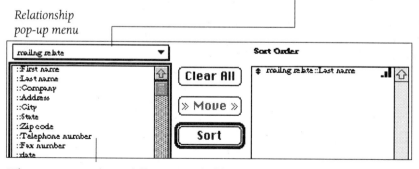

When you sort a relational file, you see double colons (::) in front of the names. The main file is then not sorted.

Sorting relational databases

■ Finding records

Finding records means looking through the database and finding information that matches a criterion or test: for example, finding all people in a mailing list who live in California.

The Find mode screen

In Find mode, an empty layout appears on screen. You type what you wish to find in the appropriate blank field.

You can still switch layouts using the layouts pop-up menu in this mode.

The blank fields are where you type in what it is you need to find.

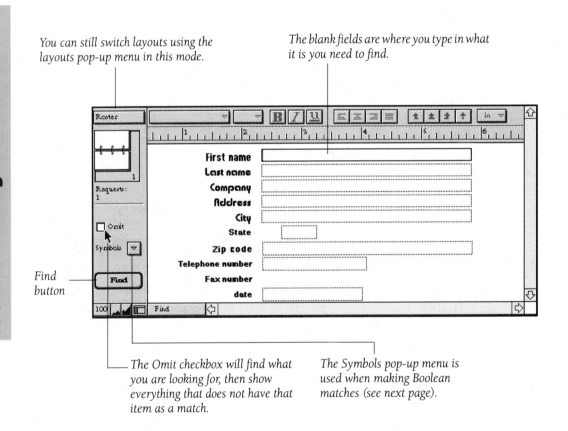

Find button

The Omit checkbox will find what you are looking for, then show everything that does not have that item as a match.

The Symbols pop-up menu is used when making Boolean matches (see next page).

Performing a simple find

A simple find allows you to type information into only one field. To look for two or more items simultaneously, see "Complex searches" on page 128.

To perform a simple find:

1. Choose *Find* from the Mode menu, or press ⌘-**F**. The layout appears with a Find button on the left-hand side of the layout.
2. In the field that contains the type of information you are looking for, type the exact item you want to find (for example, California).
3. Click the Find button. The Rolodex status area reflects exactly how many records were found.

Boolean matches

Using the Symbols pop-up menu to create a Boolean match is a more precise way to look for things. The symbols are selected just after you click in the field you need to search, but before you type the information you wish to find into the blank field.

To perform a Boolean match:

1. Choose *Find* from the Mode menu, or press ⌘-**F**. The layout appears with a Find button on the left-hand side of the layout.
2. Select the field that contains the type of information you are looking for.
3. Click the Symbols button and select the symbol that helps you best limit your search. The symbol appears in the blank field.
4. In the field, directly after the symbol, type the exact item you want to find (for example, California).
5. Click the Find button. The Rolodex status area reflects exactly how many records were found.

What FileMaker Pro 3 looks for...

How precise do you have to be when you type in the information you are looking for? FileMaker Pro 3 checks for:

▲ *A match, but capitalization might be different; for example: you type* mr., *it finds Mr.*

▲ *A match that contains the information, even if the information is buried in a word; for example: you type* bed, *it finds Bedford*

<	**Less than**
≤	**Less than or equal**
>	**greater than**
≥	**greater than or equal**
=	**exact match**
...	**range**
!	**duplicates**
//	**today's date**
?	**Invalid date or time**
@	**One character**
*	**zero or more characters**
""	**Literal text**

First name	=Kathryn Grayson

Here is a field with the equal symbol and a name typed in. This is how searches should look: first the symbol, then the information.

First name	!Char

Here's how you look for duplicates. The symbol is the exclamation mark (!). Once you've found duplicates, then you can delete them using Delete All from the Mode menu.

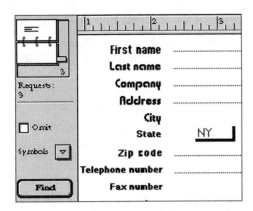

✔ **Tip:** *To see your previous request screens, use the Rolodex to move back and forth between each simultaneous request. You can edit the search that way. This search is three requests.*

✔ **Warning:** *New Request looks for alternate information, an either/or type of situation. If you want to strictly limit your search to two sets of facts, such as people who live in California (state) and Berkeley (city), type both of those facts in the same request screen.*

■ Complex searches

In complex searches, you look for two alternative sets of facts simultaneously: for example, all people who live in California and also people who live in New York.

You can make this type of a find as complicated as you want. Just repeat step 3.

To perform a complex find:

1. Choose *Find* from the Mode menu, or press ⌘-**F**. The layout appears with a Find button on the left-hand side of the layout.
2. In the field that contains the type of information you are looking for, type the first piece of information you want to find (for example, `California`).
3. Choose *New Request* from the Mode menu, or press ⌘-**N**. A new request screen appears.
4. In this second request screen, type the second piece of information you are looking for (for example, `Oakland`).
5. Click the Find button. The Rolodex status area reflects exactly how many records were found.

Mode	
Browse	⌘B
✓Find	⌘F
Layout	⌘L
Preview	⌘U
New Request	⌘N
Duplicate Request	⌘D
Delete Request	⌘E
Delete All	
Sort...	⌘S
Replace...	⌘=
Relookup	
Revert Request	

Request commands

Type of command	What it does
New Request ⌘-**N**	Creates a new request screen for searching for a second set of facts
Duplicate Request ⌘-**D**	Creates a copy of the previous request screen including the contents
Delete Request ⌘-**E**	Deletes the request screen that is currently showing
Revert Request	Changes the current screen back to whatever screen and contents directly preceded it

■ Finding a range of records

Sometimes you need to find records that fall into a certain range, for example all employees hired between two dates or all products in a particular price range.

To perform a range find:

1. Choose *Find* from the Mode menu, or press ⌘-**F**. The layout appears with a Find button on the left-hand side of the layout.

2. In the field that contains the type of information you are looking for, type the first number in the range of information you want to find (for example, the start of a zip code range such as 94600).

3. Choose the range symbol from the Symbols pop-up menu. The range symbol resembles an ellipsis, or three dots in a row. The symbol appears directly after the first piece of information you entered.

4. Still in that field, type the last number in the range of information you are looking for (for example, the end of a zip code range such as 94699).

5. Click the Find button. The Rolodex status area reflects exactly how many records were found.

<	**Less than**
≤	**Less than or equal**
>	**greater than**
≥	**greater than or equal**
=	**exact match**
...	**range**
!	**duplicates**
//	**today's date**
?	**Invalid date or time**
⊕	**One character**
*	**zero or more characters**
«»	**Literal text**

Zip code ┊94600...94699┊

This is a sample of how a range search should look when entered. Notice the range symbol between the two numbers. This search finds records containing the lowest number, 94600, and all numbers that are between it and the highest number, 94699—including 94699.

```
◄  Less than
≤  Less than or equal
►  greater than
≥  greater than or equal
=  exact match
... range
!  duplicates
// today's date
?  Invalid date or time
◉  One character
*  zero or more characters
‹›‹  Literal text
```

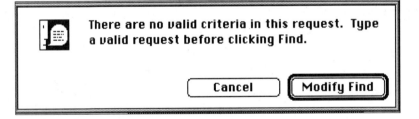

First name	=
Last name	
Company	

■ Finding blank fields

1. Choose *Find* from the Mode menu, or press ⌘-F. The layout appears with a Find button on the left-hand side of the layout.
2. Select the field you suspect might have blank entries in it.
3. Choose the equal (=) symbol from the Symbols pop-up list. Do not enter anything after the equal sign.
4. Click the Find button. The Rolodex status area reflects exactly how many records were found.

■ Search warnings

If FileMaker Pro 3 doesn't like what you have typed in as a search request, you will see a warning box. You need to go back and modify your Find request by clicking the Modify Find button.

> There are no valid criteria in this request. Type a valid request before clicking Find.
>
> Cancel   Modify Find

■ Using the search results

Once you have found your records, you have several options for using the information you have just found.

Finding all records

If you just conducted a search, you have access only to the found set of records. To use all of the records in the database, you need to find all of the records. There is a shortcut to do this.

▲ In the Browse mode, choose *Find All* from the Select menu, or press ⌘-**J**. All of your records now appear in the Rolodex status area.

Switching sets of information

What happens if you found a set of records, but what you really need is all of the records that weren't found? You need to switch sets of information:

▲ Choose *Find Omitted* from the Select menu. The set that was initially found will be hidden, and the set that wasn't initially found will be available for use.

*Need to get back to your entire database? Choose Find All, or press ⌘-**J**.*

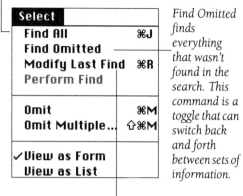

Find Omitted finds everything that wasn't found in the search. This command is a toggle that can switch back and forth between sets of information.

*If you want to modify or change the criterion in your last Find request, choose Modify Last Find from the Select menu, or press ⌘-**R**.*

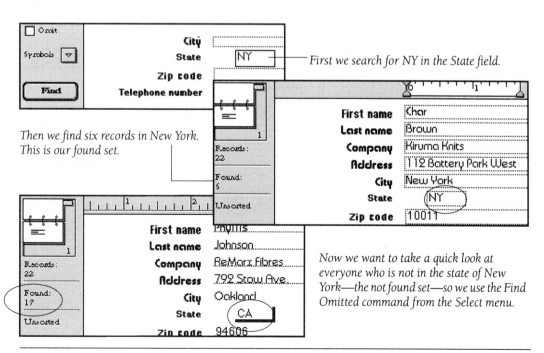

First we search for NY in the State field.

Then we find six records in New York. This is our found set.

Now we want to take a quick look at everyone who is not in the state of New York—the not found set—so we use the Find Omitted command from the Select menu.

Using the search results

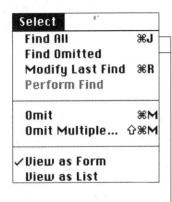

Omitting is not deleting, but rather temporarily hiding a record or records and moving them back into the not found portion of the database.

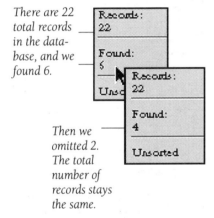

There are 22 total records in the database, and we found 6.

Then we omitted 2. The total number of records stays the same.

■ Omitting records

Omitting a record from a found set

If you're looking through your database and all of a sudden you find a record you wish hadn't been found, you can eliminate that record from the found set without deleting it. It then will become part of the not found set.

To omit a record from a found set:

▲ With the record you wish to omit in front of you on screen, choose *Omit* from the Select menu, or press ⌘-M. The current record will become part of the not found record set.

Omitting more than one record from a found set

1. With the first record you wish to omit in front of you on screen, choose *Omit Multiple* from the Select menu. The Omit Multiple dialog box appears.
2. In the omit box, type in how many records you wish to omit, counting the current record on screen as record number one.
3. Click the Omit button when you are finished.

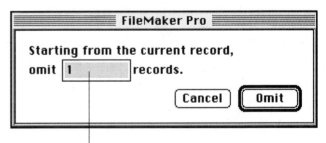

Type the number of records that you wish to omit in the omit box, counting the record on screen as the first record.

■ Deleting found information

You can delete one record or the entire found set.

To delete one record:

▲ With the record from the found set that you wish to delete on screen, choose *Delete Record* from the Mode menu, or press ⌘-**E**. The record is deleted immediately.

To delete the entire found set:

1. With the found set on screen in the Browse mode, choose *Delete All* from the Mode menu. The Delete dialog box appears.

2. Click the Delete button if you wish to delete the number of records listed in the Delete dialog box;
or
Click the Cancel button if you wish to not delete these records.

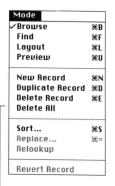

FileMaker Pro 3 will give you a warning when you choose Delete All from the Mode menu.

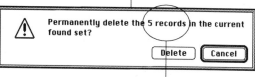

FileMaker gives you an exact count of what you are about to delete.

Deleting found information

133

Scripts & buttons

■ Automation in FileMaker Pro 3

There are two types of automation available in FileMaker Pro 3: scripts and buttons. Scripts are a form of macro; you spell out the steps you want the script to take in the ScriptMaker™, and later you play the steps back. Scripts appear on a Script menu or are assigned to keys.

Buttons can perform simple actions, such as printing, or perform scripts. Buttons appear in the layout as three-dimensional objects with a text name on top for easy identification.

ScriptMaker Define Scripts dialog box

List of created scripts

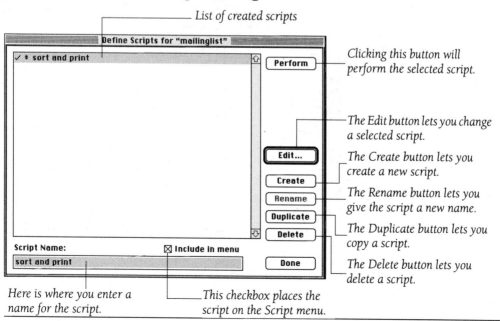

Clicking this button will perform the selected script.

The Edit button lets you change a selected script.

The Create button lets you create a new script.

The Rename button lets you give the script a new name.

The Duplicate button lets you copy a script.

The Delete button lets you delete a script.

Here is where you enter a name for the script.

This checkbox places the script on the Script menu.

■ Creating a script

We will create a sample script that first performs a sort, then prints the database.

To create a script:

Scripting tips

▲ *Before you create a script, run through the actions yourself manually.*

▲ *Write each step down as you perform it the first time so you won't miss a single action. With more experience you won't need to do this.*

▲ *Refer to your written list as you construct the script, making sure you leave none of the steps out.*

1. Choose *ScriptMaker* from the Script menu. (You can be in any mode to do this.) The Define Scripts dialog box appears.

2. Type a name for the script in the Script Name box. We used the name Sort and Print for the example script.

3. Click the Create button. The Script Definition dialog box appears.

4. Click the Clear All button to remove any current script actions from the action list.

5. Double-click the action you want the script to take from the Available Steps scrolling list.

6. Add any other actions you want the script to take and click the OK button in the Script Definition dialog box when you are done.

7. Click the Done button in the Define Scripts dialog box when you are finished.

This is the action box that lists the actions in the order you want them to be performed.

The Available Steps scrolling list gives you all of the actions a script can perform. You need to select them in the proper order.

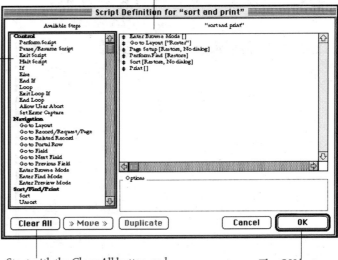

Start with the Clear All button and remove any existing scripting information from the action box.

The OK button

Creating a script

■ Editing a script

Need to make changes? No problem.

To edit a script:

1. Choose *ScriptMaker* from the Script menu. The Define Scripts dialog box appears.
2. Select the script you wish to edit from the Define Scripts dialog box.
3. Click the Edit button. The Script Definition dialog box appears.
4. Perform any of the actions you need to use from the table below.
5. Click the OK button in the Script Definition dialog box when you are done.
6. Click the Done button in the Define Scripts dialog box when you are finished.

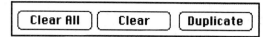

These are the buttons you use when you edit a script. They are located near the bottom of the Script Definition dialog box.

Editing actions

What you want to do	How to do it
Remove one action from the action list	1. Select the action in the action list. 2. Click the Clear button.
Remove all actions from the action list	Click the Clear All button.
Move an action up or down the list	1. Select the action. 2. Drag the action to the new position.
Copy an action	1. Select the action in the action list. 2. Click the Duplicate button.
Insert a new action	1. Double-click the action from the Available Steps list. The action appears at the bottom of the action list. 2. Drag the action to the new position.

Editing a script

```
┌─────────────────────────┐
│ Script                  │
├─────────────────────────┤
│ ScriptMaker™...         │
├─────────────────────────┤
│ sort and print    ⌘1    │
└─────────────────────────┘
```

If you have selected the Include in menu checkbox in the Define Scripts dialog box, the script will appear on this menu. FileMaker Pro 3 assigns a shortcut key to each script.

✔ **Tip:** *To stop a script, try the solutions in this order:*
1. ⌘-. (period).
2. Turn the printer off using the Print-Monitor.
3. Really desperate? Turn the printer off and wait at least 10 or 15 seconds.

Playing a script *(sidebar)*

■ Playing a script

Once you have created your script, you need to play it back in order to use it. Scripts are saved with the file, so the next time you open up a FileMaker Pro 3 file, your script will still be there.

To play back a script:

▲ Select the script you want to play from the Script menu, *or*

▲ Use the shortcut key that has been assigned automatically to the script, *or*

▲ Choose *ScriptMaker* from the Script menu, select the script from the Define Scripts dialog box, and click the Perform button.

Stopping a script that is playing

You'd better be quick! Most scripts will play so quickly you won't be able to stop them.

A couple of tricks might help you here:

▲ If you've sent a print signal to the printer in your script and you really don't want to print, try using the PrintMonitor to stop printing.

▲ The ⌘-. (period) combination will stop whatever is going on in your script if you have inserted the script command Allow User Abort [on] at the beginning of the script before you run the script.

▲ Anytime your script calls up a dialog box with a Cancel button, select the Cancel button. This tip will always work.

Bear in mind a couple of things influence how fast something such as sorting or printing actually happens: the speed of your machine as determined by the chip model, the amount of RAM your machine has, and believe it or not, the length of the cable going from your machine to your printer or other peripheral if you are printing.

Once a signal has been sent to your printer or your modem, you can't always cancel it easily. The signal is over there and you are still here, sitting in front of your keyboard, wishing the modem wouldn't dial or the printer wouldn't print.

■ Script refinements

Some script action choices require you to select
other information in order to complete the action.
Here are some examples.

Available Steps actions

Available Steps action	What it does	What you do
Perform Script	Performs a script in the middle of the current script	Select the script you want performed from the Specify pop-up menu at the bottom of the Script Definition dialog box.
Pause/Resume Script	Stops a script indefinitely or temporarily	Select the option from the Specify pop-up menu at the bottom of the Script Definition dialog box.
Go to Layout	Moves from one layout to another layout	Select the layout the script is to move to from the Specify pop-up menu at the bottom of the Script Definition dialog box.
Sort	Sorts database	Select one or both of the choices in checkboxes at the bottom of the Script Definition dialog box: Restore sort order when finished and/or Perform without seeing the Sort dialog box.
Dial Phone	Dials modem	Select the phone number from the Dial Phone dialog box from the Specify pop-up menu at the bottom of the Script Definition dialog box.

■ Using script refinements

The illustration below shows you how you can tell whether or not you need to take another step to make your script work:

1. In the Script Definition dialog box, click once on the command that has square brackets [ ] after it. The script refinements appear in the Options panel of the dialog box.

2. Select the checkbox options or choose an item from any pop-up list in the Options panel. The choices will be different depending on the exact script command.

When you see a script command that has square brackets [ ] to the right of it, that is the signal that additional refinements are available to you.

Square brackets [ ] show the choices you have made in the options panel.

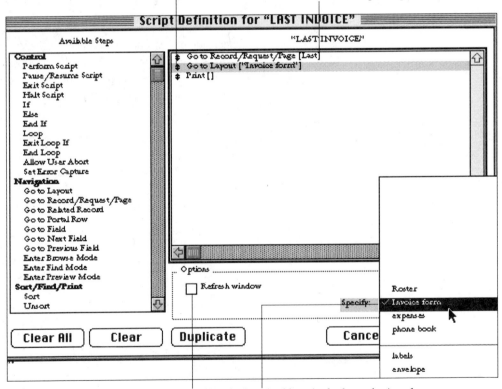

This command has both a checkbox (Refresh window) and a pop-up menu. Since this is the Go to Layout command, the pop-up menu lists all of the available layouts.

■ A complex script example

This example shows you how to use the options that frequently accompany certain command choices in the ScriptMaker (see "Script refinements" on page 139).

Pausing a script

This script pauses and lets you perform some data entry in the last record; then you tell the script to start back up, and the script sorts the data:

1. Choose *ScriptMaker* from the Script menu. The Define Scripts dialog box appears.
2. Type a name for the script in the Script Name box.
3. Click the Create button.
4. Choose the *Enter Browse Mode* command from the Navigation section of the Available Steps scrolling list.
5. Choose the *Go to Layout* command from the Navigation section of the Available Steps scrolling list. An option appears in the Options panel.
6. Select the Layout you wish the script to move to from the Specify pop-up menu.
7. Choose the *Go to Record/Request/Page* command from the Navigation section of the Available Steps scrolling list. An option appears in the Options panel.
8. Select the record you wish the script to move to from the Specify pop-up menu. This example used the Last record from this list.
9. Choose the *Pause/Resume Script* command from the Control section of the Available Steps scrolling menu.
10. Choose the *Sort* command from the Sort/Find/Print section of the Available Steps scrolling menu.
11. Click the OK button when you are done. A Sort Order dialog box may appear. If it does, click the OK button in that dialog box.
12. Click the Done button in the Define Scripts dialog box.

The choices that are made in the Specify pop-up box appear in brackets after the command.

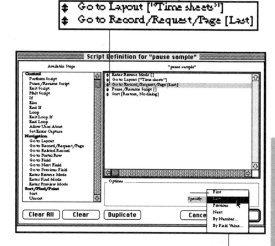

This is the Specify pop-up list in the Options panel for the Go to Record/Request/Page command. If you need to make a change to the Specify pop-up list, double-click the command in the script scrolling list.

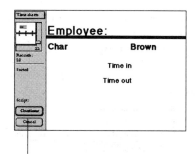

When you play the script, a Continue button appears on the left side of the screen. Click this button when you are ready for the script to continue.

A complex script example

■ Printing a script

You can print your layouts (see Chapter 14, "Printing & Help," on page 175), scripts, or field definitions in this new version of FileMaker Pro. Printing scripts and field definitions gives you documentation so you can remember what it is you did when you set up that marvelous accounting program.

To print a script:

1. Select the printer you wish to use from the Chooser in the Apple menu. If you change printers from the last time you printed using FileMaker Pro 3, recheck your Page Setup options.

2. Choose *Print* from the File menu, or press ⌘-P. The Print dialog box appears.

3. Select the Script radio button in the Print area of the Print dialog box.

4. If you want to print just one script, select the script you want to print from the Script pop-up menu.

5. Click the Print button.

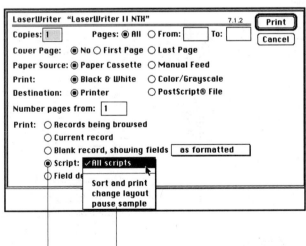

This is the Print dialog box for a LaserWriter. Here is where you select the script you want to print. Your Print dialog box might be a little different.

Printing a script

■ What are buttons?

Buttons are rectangular objects that start a script or perform a simple action when you click them. You can create these buttons, place them in your layout, then specify that they not print. That way you can conveniently use them, but they won't mess up the printout.

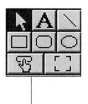

Use the button tool to create a button. Click the button tool then drag the pointer until you have a button the size and shape you like.

Creating a basic button

1. In the Layout mode, click the button tool in the tool panel.
2. In the layout, drag the pointer until the button is the desired size. The Specify Button dialog box appears.
3. Double-click the action you want the button to perform from the Specify Button scrolling list.
4. If any options you want to use appear in the Options panel, select them.
5. Click the OK button when you are finished. The blinking cursor appears in the middle of the button.
6. Type a name for the button.
7. Click outside of the button to finish.

Here is the list of actions you can choose from. Double-click the action you want to have the button perform.

The Specify Button dialog box presents options for the selected action. Use the pop-up menu to select the correct option.

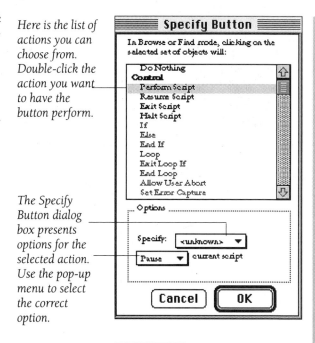

The finished button

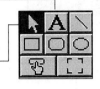

Use the text tool to edit the button name and use the pointer tool to make the button smaller or larger.

With the text tool, drag over the button name, then type the new text.

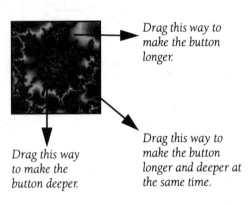

Drag this way to make the button longer.

Drag this way to make the button deeper.

Drag this way to make the button longer and deeper at the same time.

■ Changing buttons

Editing a button name

1. In the Layout mode, select the text tool from the toolbox.
2. Drag the pointer over the text you wish to change.
3. Type the changes, including changing the font, font size, and font enhancements.
4. Click outside of the button when you are finished.

Changing the button size

1. In the Layout mode, select the pointer tool from the toolbox.
2. Click the button you wish to change.
3. Drag one of the button handles until the button is the correct size.
4. Click outside of the button when you are finished.

■ Buttons, colors, and fills

Just because it's a nice gray, three-dimensional button doesn't mean it can't become a lively, colorful button filled with a pattern.

To change the appearance of a button:

1. In the Layout mode, select the button you wish to change.
2. Select one of the tools from the chart below to enhance the button.

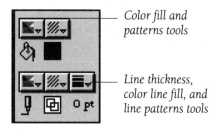

Color fill and patterns tools

Line thickness, color line fill, and line patterns tools

You aren't stuck with the default choices for buttons in FileMaker Pro 3. Use the tools for color and pattern to dress up those plain gray buttons.

Color and text actions

What you want to do	How to do it
Make the button background a color	1. Select the button. 2. Click the color fill button in the tools palette. 3. Select a color from the color fill palette.
Change the line around the button	1. Select the button. 2. Click the line thickness button in the tools palette. 3. Select the line size you want to use.
Create a colored line around the button.	1. Select the button. 2. Select the color line fill button from the tools palette. 3. Select a color from the line color palette.
Change the color of the text in a button.	1. Select the button. 2. Choose *Text Color* from the Format menu. 3. Select a color from the text color palette.
Change the typeface on a button.	1. Select the button. 2. Choose *Font* or *Text* from the Format menu. 3. Select the font you want the button to have.

Buttons, colors, and fills

This is the action to choose from the Specify Button scrolling list.

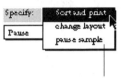

The Specify pop-up menu gives you a list of all available scripts.

■ Putting a script on a button

Linking a script and a button requires just one more step than creating a basic button.

To link a script and a button:

1. In the Layout mode, click the button tool in the tool panel.

2. In the layout, drag the pointer until the button is the desired size. The Specify Button dialog box appears.

3. Double-click the Perform Script action in the Control section of the Specify Button scrolling list.

4. Select the script you want the button to perform from the Specify pop-up menu.

5. Click the OK button when you are finished. The blinking cursor appears in the button.

6. Type a name for the button.

7. Click outside of the button to finish.

Making buttons nonprinting

Buttons are handy, buttons are cool—but not in the middle of a nice printout. Here's how you keep those buttons from printing:

Select this checkbox and the button does not print.

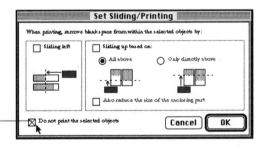

1. In the Layout mode, select the button you don't want to print.

2. Choose *Sliding/Printing* from the Format menu, or press Option-⌘-T. The Set Sliding/Printing dialog box appears.

3. Select the Do not print the selected objects checkbox at the bottom of the Set Sliding/Printing dialog box.

4. Click the OK button.

Putting a script on a button

■ Making a fancy button

While FileMaker Pro makes perfectly good buttons that can be filled with colors and patterns just like other objects, you can create buttons of your own from drawings you have made.

Go wild!

Use your clip art, your scanner—anything to make an interesting button. Turn a favorite saying into a button. Make your least favorite person a punching button!

Fancy buttons were created using Adobe Photoshop 3.0 as follows:
Top row, left to right

- ▲ *Kai's Power Tools Fractal Explorer 2.0*
- ▲ *Scanned portrait of writer at age three with father*
- ▲ *Scanned image of pin created by Oakland, California, artist Joe Sam, original art owned by the San Francisco Art Commission*

Bottom row, left to right

- ▲ *Scanned brass template*
- ▲ *Scanned embroidered Hmong purse*
- ▲ *Kai's Power Tools Extensions Page Curl*

To make your own art into a button:

1. In the Layout mode, place the drawing you have made.
2. Select the drawing.
3. Choose *Button* from the Format menu. The Specify Button dialog box appears.
4. Select the action you want the new button to take from the scrolling list.
5. If an option appears in the Options panel, select any checkboxes you wish to use or make any necessary choice from the pop-up menu.
6. Click the OK button when you are done. The piece of art, your drawing or object, is now a button.

The Specify Button dialog box really works with any selected object.

■ Sample scripts and buttons

Buttons and scripts can simplify many complex operations by automating some actions. Use the suggestions given here as a starting point for your own time-saving innovations.

Color-code the buttons so they will be easier to spot. Use the color fill tool in the tool panel.

This button goes to the invoice entry screen. Choose Go to Layout in the Specify Button scrolling list, then pick the layout from the pop-up menu in the Options panel.

This button uses a script that goes to the Find layout, pauses for entry, performs the find, switches to the customer information screen for the customer, and waits for data entry. When the data entry is finished, the script then prints the layout.

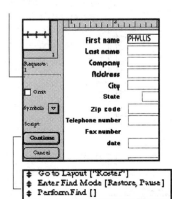

Priddy's Products Opening Menu

CUSTOMER ENTRY

SALES ENTRY

PRINT INVOICE

TIME CLOCK

This button uses a simple script command that moves to the last invoice that was created and then prints it.

This button moves to the time clock layout that contains a formula to calculate employee time. See "Finding how much time has passed" on page 120 for instructions.

Script for the Print Invoice button

Time sheet layout

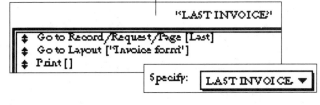

Invoice Number	2122
Date	2/8/96
Terms	Net 30
Payment due	3/9/96

Time worked
Time out - Time in

Relational concepts

■ Relational terms

Before you begin thinking about relational
databases, you need to know a few general terms,
and you need to understand why you would ever
want to use a relational database.

Why relational?

Relational databases save disk space, speed up data
entry options, and reduce the chance of data entry
error by borrowing information from a central
location. You enter your customers' names once
in a customer database, and when you create orders
for these customers, instead of entering their names
again, you *borrow* them from the original entry.

Current database

The *current* database is the database you see on
screen. This database is the database that is
borrowing information.

Related database

The *related* database is the database that information is borrowed from. You won't see this one
on screen, although this file is always open in the
background.

Linking field

A *linking field* has the same name as a field in the
related database. When information is entered into
the current database's linking field, FileMaker Pro
3 looks that information up and borrows any information you need.

*Before you begin designing your relational file, dip
into the simple terminology on the left so you will
understand what this chapter is all about!*

✔ **Important:** *Having a field in common is what makes relational databases work.*

■ What does relational mean?

Relational databases are databases that borrow information from each other by having one field in common. It works like this (one picture in this case is really worth a thousand words):

This customer database contains all of the customer information. The common field is the Customer ID Number.

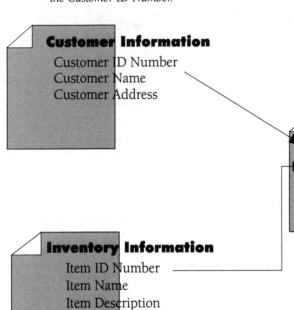

This current database contains all of the customer order information. When the Customer ID Number is typed in, all of the other customer information automatically appears in the Customer Orders database.

Customer Information
Customer ID Number
Customer Name
Customer Address

Customer Orders
Customer ID Number
Item ID Number
Quantity Ordered
Customer Address

Inventory Information
Item ID Number
Item Name
Item Description
Price
Quantity In Stock

When the Item ID Number is typed in, the name, description, and price information is borrowed from the Inventory Information database. No more retyping or guessing!

Like the Customer Information database, the Inventory Information database contains a common field with the Customer Orders database.

■ How relationships work

The key to relating one database to another is linking fields. Borrowed information isn't actually imported into the current database, but appears there as a sort of electronic illusion.

✔ **Tip:** *The current database is the database that needs to borrow information from its relations. A current database could act as a relation to other databases.*

This customer database shows a Customer ID number of UCH32 for a particular client. When the Customer ID number is typed in the invoice–order entry database, the rest of the customer information such as the address, city, state, and zip code is borrowed from the customer database.

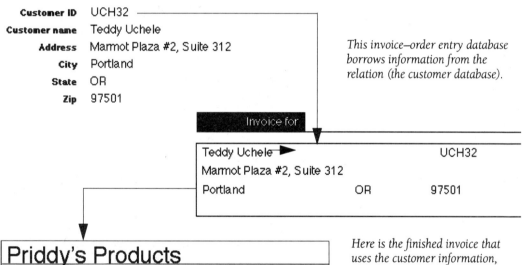

This invoice–order entry database borrows information from the relation (the customer database).

Here is the finished invoice that uses the customer information, plus the item description and price from another relational file. The Item identification number is the linking field that helps the invoice borrow the description and price information, while the quantity is typed in. The extension and grand total are calculated fields based on the quantity (an entered field) and price (a borrowed field) entries.

How relationships work

151

■ Making decisions

When do you need a relational database? Use the table below to help you make a decision.

Going relational

Once you complete the decision-making process, you can choose between two methods of relating information: defining relationships and setting up portals. If you have used FileMaker Pro 2, defining relationships should remind you of the way FileMaker Pro 2 borrowed information.

Relational database decision making

Situation	Examples
Do you use information in a field more than once?	Inventory numbers, items to be ordered from an inventory
Could you use information that is in one database in another database?	Customer names, addresses, account numbers
Do a variety of actions happen to something that is in a database?	Accounts payable, payment schedules, accounts receivable, inventory received and shipped
Does the proposed database seem as if it may become a very large database?	Any type of common element between entries, such as a standard fee, sales tax, shared addresses
Do you need to look at data from another database, but not necessarily use the data?	Membership rosters, event planning, common scripted buttons

■ Getting organized

Going relational means doing some homework. Here are steps that will help you make a clean relational database:

1. Describe the main point of your database in one sentence or less. Is it to track inventory? To make sure everyone pays dues? To invoice customers? Keep track of appointments in an office?

2. List all of the fields for each related database, putting each list in a separate column.

3. Find one field in each column that can act as a linking field. It could be an identification number, though sometimes, not always, telephone numbers will work. Social security numbers or invoice numbers are an excellent source of unique identification also. Circle that one field in each column. Place the linking field in each column that will need to borrow information.

4. The columns will become your databases. The fields within the columns that are not circled will become plain fields.

5. The circled fields will become the linking fields that help pull in information from another database.

6. Everything else is plain old data entry!

7. Place a title for each column based on the function of the set of related columnar information.

✔ **Tip:** *The point of relational databases is to not have to constantly be retyping information that you can reuse.*

Sample organizational chart for an order entry system

Customers	Inventory	Sales	Payment
Name	Item	Item	Customer information
(ID number)	(ID number)	Item ID number	(Invoice number)
Address	Description	Description	Amount due
City, state, zip code	Quantity on hand	Quantity	Amount paid
Telephone/fax numbers	Wholesale price	Price	Type of payment (cash, credit card, refund)
Shipping address	Retail price	Shipping method	Payment date
Number of previous sales	Quantity received from wholesale house	Customer information	Individual item information
		(Customer ID number)	Shipping information
		Invoice number	

Getting organized

Next steps

Once you have your organizational chart, you begin designing your database. Based on the sample organizational chart on page 153, you have the following databases:

- ▲ Customers database
- ▲ Inventory database
- ▲ Sales database
- ▲ Payment database

Each database represents one column in your organizational layout.

Each database must have one field in common (the circled items on the sample organizational chart).

All other fields in each database must be entirely different (the uncircled items on the chart).

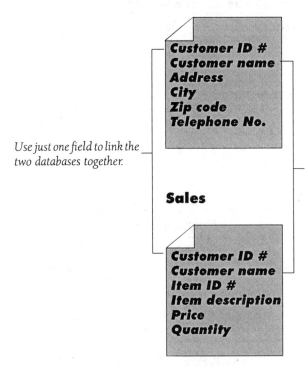

Customers

Customer ID #
Customer name
Address
City
Zip code
Telephone No.

Use just one field to link the two databases together.

If you're planning on typing the Customer name into the Sales database, don't. The point of relational databases is that this information is borrowed.

Sales

Customer ID #
Customer name
Item ID #
Item description
Price
Quantity

■ Getting started

Now that you've gotten a brief idea of how relational databases work (see page 149), let's get started creating our first relational database.

Before you start, make sure:
▲ You have two databases (at least)
▲ Each database has one field that has the same name and is the same field type. This is the field the databases will use to link together and form a relationship.

To define a relationship:

1. In the Layout mode of the current database, choose *Define Relationships* from the File menu. The Define Relationships dialog box appears.
2. Click the New button. The File name dialog box appears.
3. Double-click the file name you want to link to your current database. The Edit Relationship dialog box appears.
4. Select the field of your current file that you want to designate as the linking field in the Match data from field in current file scrolling list.
5. Select the linking field of the relational file from which you want to borrow the information in the With data from field in related file scrolling list.
6. Click the OK button. The Define Relationships dialog box reappears.
7. Click the Done button.

It all starts here with Define Relationships.

You need to click the New button to start a new relationship. The scrolling list will show any existing relationships.

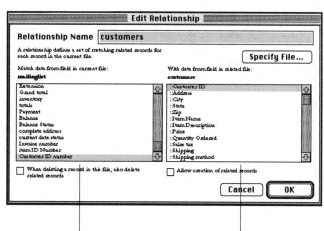

The current file list represents the fields in the current database.

The related file list represents the fields in the relational database.

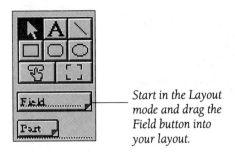

Start in the Layout mode and drag the Field button into your layout.

■ Using a related field

Now that you have established a link, you need to use the related fields in your current file.

To use a field in a related file:

1. In the Layout mode, drag the Field button from the tool palette into the layout. The Specify Field dialog box appears.

2. Select the related file from the pop-up menu at the top of the Specify Field dialog box. The list of the related file's fields appears in the scrolling list. Each field name is preceded by a double colon.

3. Select the field you want to use from the list and click the OK button. Don't forget to select the Create field label checkbox if you want a field label created at the same time.

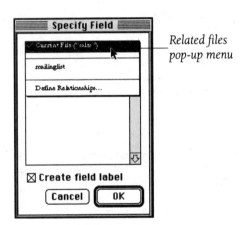

Related files pop-up menu

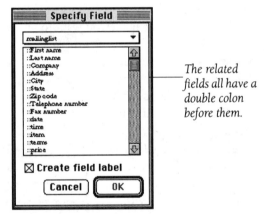

The related fields all have a double colon before them.

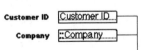

One regular field and one related field—the layout shows you the double colons before the field name as a clue.

4. Drag the relational field to the correct position in the layout.

5. Repeat steps 1 through 4 for any additional fields you wish to use from the related file.

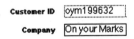

■ Entering data

▲ In the Browse mode of the current database, enter information into the linking field that you know is in the related file. The rest of the related information should appear.

A couple of related file options enhance how data can be entered in the current database.

Related file options

Two of the options at the bottom of the Edit Relationship dialog box enable FileMaker Pro 3 to create a record in the related file when the information is entered into the current file, or to delete information in the related file when information is deleted in the current file.

To use related file options:

1. In the Layout mode of the current database, choose *Define Relationships* from the File menu. The Define Relationships dialog box appears.
2. Select the relationship you wish to change from the Define Relationships dialog box.
3. Click the Edit button. The Edit Relationship dialog box appears.

4. Select the When deleting a record in this file checkbox and the Allow creation of related records checkbox from the bottom of the Edit Relationship dialog box.
5. Click the OK button.

Testing the options

In your current database, enter a completely new record. Open your related database and the information should appear.

Pitfalls...

Did it work when you entered data? Did your related information show up? It should have, unless:

▲ *The linking field names were not the same*

▲ *The linking field types were not the same*

There are the two checkboxes at the bottom of the Edit Relationship dialog box. They speed up data entry when you have new customers, items, or other related material to be entered and you know it isn't in the related file.

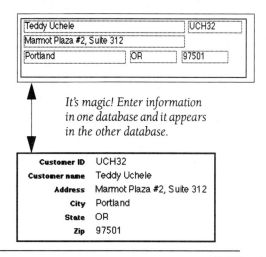

It's magic! Enter information in one database and it appears in the other database.

Customer ID	UCH32
Customer name	Teddy Uchele
Address	Marmot Plaza #2, Suite 312
City	Portland
State	OR
Zip	97501

■ Relational math

This example multiplies two fields together. One field is in the current database, the second field is in the related file.

To use a field from a related file in a calculation:

1. In the Layout mode, choose *Define Fields* from the File menu. The Define Fields dialog box appears.

2. Type a name for the field in the Field Name box.

3. Select the Calculation radio button, or press ⌘-c, then click the Create button. The Specify Calculation dialog box appears.

4. Select the name of the related database file from the pop-up menu at the top of the field name scrolling list. The items in the field name scrolling list change to the field names of the related file. Each field name has a double colon in front of it.

5. Select the field name you wish to use.

6. Select the mathematical symbol you wish to use from the mathematical symbols buttons.

7. Select the next field you wish to use from the field name scrolling list;
   or
   Change the file by selecting a new file name from the pop-up box at the top of the field name scrolling list.

8. Click the OK button.

For more information on creating calculations in FileMaker Pro 3, see "Creating basic calculations" on page 108.

This is the pop-up list that you use to select the related file. If you haven't yet defined the relationship, you also have a chance to choose Define Relationships from this pop-up menu.

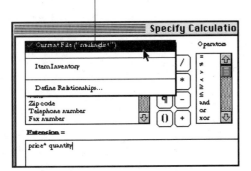

Once you have selected the related file, the scrolling field name list contains a list of the fields that are in the related file.

When related fields are used in calculations, the calculation shows the file name plus the field name. Fields from the current database just show the field name.

⬩ quantity	Number	Repeating
⬩ Cost of Goods, Gross	Number	
⬩ Extension	Calculation	Unstored, = ItemInventory::Retail price * quantity
⬩ Grand total	Summary	= Total of Extension
⬩ inventory	Text	Creator Name, Repeating
⬩ totals	Calculation	= quantity * quantity

Even the Define Fields dialog box gives you a clue that a calculation contains a related field.

■ Indexing

Indexing maps all occurrences of a field in a way that lets FileMaker Pro 3 search the field entries more efficiently. You can think of indexing as a kind of internal sorting; FileMaker Pro doesn't show you the results on screen, but does perform searches faster as a result.

Turn indexing on if you want to:
▲ Find information in a database faster
▲ Use unique field entries

To turn indexing on:

1. In the Layout mode, choose *Define Fields* from the File menu. The Define Fields dialog box appears.
2. Select the field name you want to index.
3. Click the Options button. The Entry Options dialog box appears.
4. Click the Storage Options button at the bottom of either dialog box. The Storage Options dialog box appears.
5. Select the On radio button from the Indexing panel of the Storage Options dialog box.
6. Click the OK button.

Indexing and calculated fields

You can't index a calculated field. When you select Storage Options for a calculated field, the choice you have is to store or not to store the calculated result.

▲ Use the Do not store calculation results checkbox in the Storage options dialog box to change this option.

The Define Fields dialog box shows you whether a field has been indexed in the Options column.

Field Name	Type	Options
↕ First name	Text	Indexed
↕ Last name	Text	Indexed
↕ Company	Text	Indexed
↕ Address	Text	

Indexing can slow down creating a new record or retrieving the file while FileMaker Pro reindexes the existing information. Finding what you are looking for will be faster if the field you are searching in is indexed.

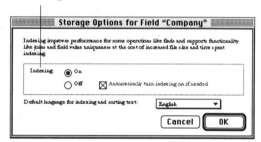

Calculated fields are not indexed. The storage options you can use with calculated fields are limited to whether or not you want to store the calculated results. Not storing the results will keep the file size smaller, but increase the time needed for data entry slightly.

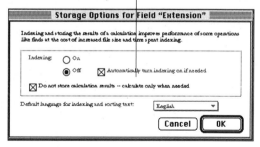

Indexing

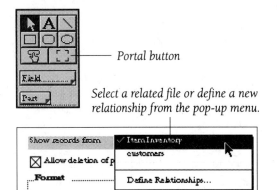

Portal button

Select a related file or define a new relationship from the pop-up menu.

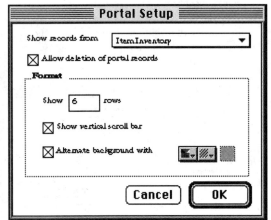

■ Portals

Portals are a way of peering into another database from an existing layout. While setting up a simple relationship allows you to select one instance of matching relationship and borrow information based on that relation, portals will let you look at all pieces of data that match a set of facts; for example, all appointments for a certain client.

Plain relationships are called one-to-one relationships. Portals are one-to-many relationships because they show more matching records from the related file.

To use a portal:

1. In the Layout mode, select the portal button from the tool palette.

2. Drag the pointer to create the size portal you want. The Portal Setup dialog box appears.

3. Select the related file from the pop-up list at the top of the Portal Setup dialog box. Portals are one form of relational field, so you must have a relationship defined. For more information on defining relationships, see "Getting started" on page 155.

4. Select any portal options you wish to use from the Format panel.

5. Click the OK button.

6. Resize the portal in the layout if necessary.

Portal options

Options	Explanation
Allow deletion of portal records	You can delete portal records while you are in the current database.
Show [number] rows	This specifies the number of rows from the portal database that show at one time in the current database.
Show vertical scroll bar	The vertical scroll bar lets you have a smaller portal that will scroll up and down the matching fields list.
Alternate background with	You can select a color and pattern for the portal background from the fill color and fill pattern buttons in the Portal Setup dialog box.

Portals

Importing & recovering data

■ Importing data

You can import information from other FileMaker Pro 3 files, older versions of FileMaker Pro, other databases, or a word processing program.

To import database files:

1. Choose *Import Records* from the Import/ Export submenu in the File menu. The Import file dialog box appears.
2. Select the file type from the Show pop-up menu. Most of the time, FileMaker Pro 3 will know what file type your file is.
3. Select the file from the file name scrolling list.
4. Click the Open button. The Import Field Mapping dialog box appears.
5. Select Matching Names from the View By pop-up list at the top of the dialog box. The field names should roughly match.
6. Click the Import button if you are satisfied. The Import options dialog box appears.
7. Select the Perform Auto-enter options checkbox if you have Auto Enter fields in your database.
8. Click the OK button.

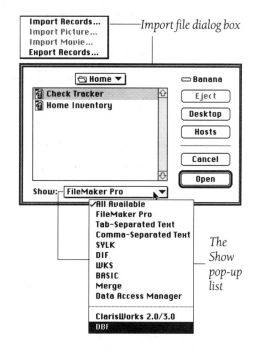

Import Records...
Import Picture...
Import Movie...
Export Records... —*Import file dialog box*

The Show pop-up list

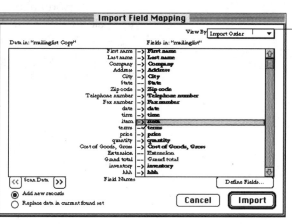

There are several viewing options in the View By pop-up list, but the option that works the best is Matching Names.

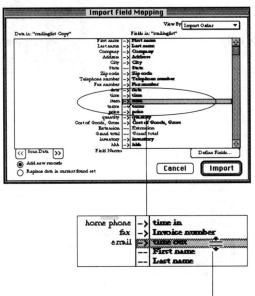

When you drag the selected fields, the cursor turns into a double-sided arrow.

■ Changing field mapping

Even if you select Matching Names from the View By pop-up list in the Import Field Mapping dialog box, things might not work out so well. You can match up any two fields by moving the fields around on the right-hand side of the dialog box.

To change field mapping:

1. Choose *Import Records* from the Import/ Export submenu in the File menu. The Import file dialog box appears.

2. Select the file type from the Show pop-up menu. Most of the time, FileMaker Pro 3 knows what file type your file is.

3. Select the file from the file name scrolling list.

4. Click the Open button. The Import Field Mapping dialog box appears.

5. Select Matching Names from the View By pop-up list at the top of the dialog box. The field names should roughly match.

6. Select the field you need to match up from the right-hand box (representing the fields in the existing file), and drag the file up to the proper position. You should be matching the file against the field names in the left-hand box (the fields being imported).

7. Click in the center where the little dashed line appears until you have an arrow pointing to the right. This activates the link.

8. Click the Import button if you are satisfied. The Import options dialog box appears.

9. Select the Perform Auto-enter options checkbox if you have Auto Enter fields in your database.

10. Click the OK button.

■ Checking data

When you first open the Import Field Mapping dialog box, the field names match in the two scrolling lists. You can change how you view the information in the left-hand scrolling list and check the field definitions for the fields in the right-hand scrolling list.

Scanning data

To change the view in the scrolling list:

1. Choose *Import Records* from the Import/Export submenu in the File menu. The Import file dialog box appears.

2. Select the file type from the Show pop-up menu. Most of the time, FileMaker Pro 3 knows what file type your file is.

3. Select the file from the file name scrolling list.

4. Click the Open button. The Import Field Mapping dialog box appears.

5. Select Matching Names from the View By pop-up list at the top of the dialog box. The field names should roughly match.

6. Click the scan button ⟩⟩ at the bottom of the Import Field Mapping dialog box. The first actual record with information appears.

7. Click the Import button if you are satisfied. The Import options dialog box appears.

8. Select the Perform Auto-enter options checkbox if you have Auto Enter fields in your database.

9. Click the OK button.

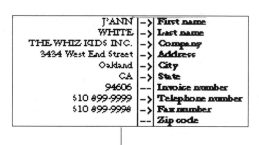

Clicking the scan button lets you view the data instead of just the field names. That way you will be sure to have the new data match the existing file's fields.

Checking data

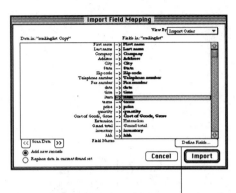

The Define Fields button lets you see what the field definitions in your existing database are.

Replace data or not?

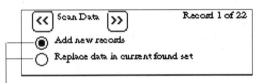

These two radio buttons determine whether you will be adding new records or replacing existing records when you import data.

Field definitions

If you need to, you can see the field definitions for the current file (the file into which you are importing the records):

1. Choose *Import Records* from the Import/ Export submenu in the File menu. The Import file dialog box appears.
2. Select the file type from the Show pop-up menu. Most of the time, FileMaker Pro 3 will know what file type your file is.
3. Select the file from the file name scrolling list.
4. Click the Open button. The Import Field Mapping dialog box appears.
5. Click the Define Fields button at the bottom of the Import Field Mapping dialog box. The Define Fields dialog box appears.
6. Click the field you want to check. For more information on the Define Fields dialog box, see "Creating fields" on page 49.
7. Click the Import button.

■ Replace data or not?

When you import records, you can choose to replace any records that are exactly the same as existing records, or you can just import the records as they stand.

To replace the records:

1. Choose *Import Records* from the Import/ Export submenu in the File menu. The Import file dialog box appears.
2. Select the file type from the Show pop-up menu. Most of the time, FileMaker Pro 3 knows what file type your file is. Click the Open button. The Import Field Mapping dialog box appears.
3. Select the file from the file name scrolling list.
4. Select the Replace data in current found set radio button at the bottom of the dialog box.
5. Click the Import button.

■ Importing from word processors

When transferring a file from any word processing program into almost any other program, it's important to get rid of the special codes that were planted there when that file was originally created.

To import a word processing file:

1. In your word processing program, use either a mail merge file, a table, or tab-separated text, and save the file as Text Only.

2. Choose *Import Records* from the Import/Export submenu in the File menu. The Import file dialog box appears.

3. Select the Tab-Separated Text file type from the Show pop-up menu if your word processed file is either tab-separated or a table originally, or Merge if your file was a merge file originally.

4. Select the file from the file name scrolling list.

5. Click the Open button. The Import Field Mapping dialog box appears. The information from your word-processed file will appear in the left-hand box. Probably nothing will be in the correct position.

6. Drag the field names in the Fields in scrolling list so they match the information.

7. Click in the center where the little dashed line appears until you have an arrow pointing to the right. This activates the link.

8. Click the Import button when you are done.

When you start out with your text in a table and then save it as Text Only, the columns become tabs. Text Only is a universal format that allows maximum flexibility in moving a file from one program to another.

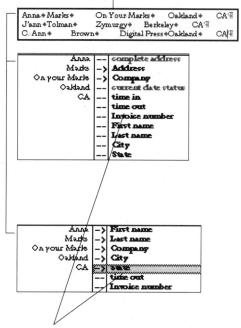

The information appears in the order in which it was typed and won't necessarily match the field names. Drag the field names around until they match the information.

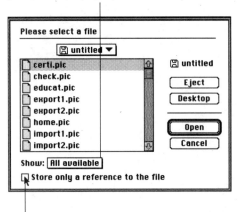

```
✓All available

AutoCAD[DHF][MacLink®]
EPSF
GIF
HarvardGraphics[CGM][MacLink®]
Lotus Freelance[CGM][MacLink®]
Lotus[PIC] [MacLink®]
MacPaint
PC PaintBrush[PCH] [MacLink®]
PICT
QuickTime Movie
TIFF
Uentura Image[IMG][MacLink®]
Uentura LineArt[GEM][MacLink®]
Windows BitMap[BMP][MacLink®]
WordPerfect Graphics[MacLink®]
```

These are the file formats that are available when you want to import a picture or movie. Select the format from the bottom of the Import dialog box.

Show pop-up menu that gives you choices for picture and movie file formats

```
Please select a file
        untitled ▼
certi.pic              untitled
check.pic
educat.pic            Eject
export1.pic          Desktop
export2.pic
home.pic             Open
import1.pic          Cancel
import2.pic

Show: All available
☐ Store only a reference to the file
```

Store only a reference checkbox

■ Importing pictures or movies

Your pictures can be in almost any format, but your movies must be in QuickTime format.

To import a picture or movie:

1. In the Layout mode, choose *Import Picture* (or *Import Movie*) from the Import/Export submenu in the File menu. The Import file dialog box appears.

2. Select the file type from the Show pop-up menu. Most of the time, FileMaker Pro 3 will know what file type your file is.

3. Select the file from the file name scrolling list.

4. Click the Open button. The picture appears in the database.

About pictures and movies

Pictures and movies can be imported into container fields. For more information on container fields, see "Container fields" on page 62. Picture fields can also be used as backgrounds, buttons, or other decorative elements on layouts. See "Adding text & graphics" on page 95 for more information about incorporating pictures or graphics into layouts.

Keeping your database small

You can keep your database small by importing pictures or movies by reference. With this option, FileMaker Pro 3 needn't incorporate a copy of the picture in the database, but can look the picture up and display it when needed.

If you store only a reference to a picture or movie, you must not move or erase the picture or movie from your hard disk, or change its name.

To store a picture or movie by reference:

▲ Select the Store only a reference to the file checkbox at the bottom of the Import file dialog box.

■ Exporting data

1. Choose *Export Records* from the Import/ Export submenu in the File menu. The Export file dialog box appears.
2. Type a new file name in the Save as box of the Export file dialog box.
3. Select the file type from the Type pop-up menu (see the column at right for some recommendations).
4. Click the Save button. The Export Field Order dialog box appears.
5. Perform any of the needed actions from the table below.
6. Click the Export button when you are done.

Just where is that file going...

These recommendations will also work if you need to transfer the file to a different platform, such as an IBM PC.

▲ *If the text is going to a word processor, separate the fields by tabs. Then you can easily transfer it into either columns or tables.*

▲ *If the text is going to another database program, a contact manager, a dialing program, or an accounting program, select the DBF format.*

▲ *If the text is going into a spreadsheet, select the WKS format.*

▲ *For other recommendations, check your target software application's technical notes.*

Exporting actions

What you want to do	How to do it
Prevent one of the fields from being exported	1. Select the field in the Field Order scrolling list. 2. Click the Clear button.
Remove all fields from the Field Order box	Click the Clear All button.
Move all fields into the Field Order box	Click the Move All button
Move an action up or down the list	1. Select the field in the Field Order scrolling list. 2. Drag the action to the new position.
Remove formatting from the output	Select the Don't format output radio button at the bottom of the Export Field Order dialog box.
Export fields from a related database	Select the file you want to export from the Current File pop-up menu at the top of the Export Field Order dialog box.
Export mathematical summary fields	1. Before you export, sort the database by at least one nonsummary field. 2. Select the field you want to export in the Field Order scrolling box. 3. Click the Summarize by button. The Summarize by dialog box appears. 4. Click the OK button. 5. Click the Export button.

Exporting data

■ Recovering data

One of the greatest strengths of FileMaker Pro 3 is the data recovery system that is in place. If you have a power surge or outage, or some little hitch in your computer that corrupts your data, FileMaker Pro 3's data recovery will most likely be able to get everything back in one piece.

▲ If you open a file that is corrupted, FileMaker Pro 3 displays a dialog box that tells you the file is being fixed. Do nothing—let FileMaker Pro 3 do the work.

> **This file was not closed properly. FileMaker is now performing a consistency check.**

This is the dialog box that FileMaker Pro 3 shows you when your file needs to be recovered. This could happen as a result of a power outage, the computer being shut off while FileMaker Pro 3 is still open, or any number of other odd little glitches that happen with computers. When you see this dialog box, FileMaker Pro 3 does all of the work for you. You just sit back and watch.

To manually recover a file:

1. Choose *Recover* from the File menu. The Recover file dialog box appears.

2. Select your file from the scrolling list.

3. Click the Open button. The File Save dialog box appears.

4. Type a new name for the recovered file in the Name box and click the Save button.

5. Click the OK button after checking the Recover dialog box to see how many files were recovered, or any potential errors.

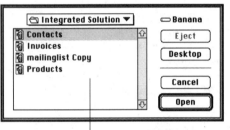

Start here and select the file you want to recover.

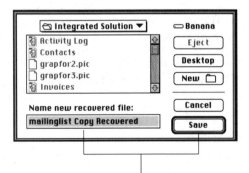

Then give the file a new name and start the recovery process by clicking the Save button.

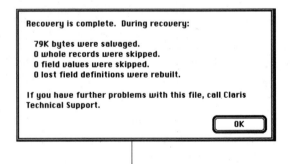

Once FileMaker Pro 3 has done all of the recovery work, this dialog box will let you know how many of your files were salvaged.

■ Translating older versions

You can translate older FileMaker Pro files into FileMaker Pro 3 simply by opening them:

1. Choose *Open* from the File menu. The Open File dialog box appears.
2. Select the file you wish to translate and click the Open button. The Conversion dialog box appears.
3. Click the OK button in the Conversion dialog box. Notice that the name in the Rename box is the same, but FileMaker Pro 3 has added the word Old at the end. This preserves the file in its original format under that name. The File Save dialog box appears.
4. Click the Save button to save the file with the same name;

   or

   Enter a new file name in the Name box and then click the Save button.

■ Moving between platforms

Good news! You can use a FileMaker Pro 3 file on the Macintosh or on a PC running Windows 95 or Windows NT with absolutely no problems.

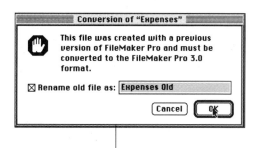

This is the Conversion dialog box that warns you the file was created with a previous version of FileMaker Pro.

Translating older versions

Mail merge

13

■ Starting a mail merge

Mail merge can be performed in FileMaker Pro 3 much like you perform a mail merge in a word processing program. The fields are placed in a special manner so that they slide with the text.

To create a mail merge:

1. In the Layout mode, choose *New Layout* from the Mode menu, or press ⌘-**L**. The New Layout dialog box appears.
2. Select the Blank radio button from the New Layout dialog box.
3. Type a name for the mail merge in the Layout Name box.
4. In the Layout, select the text tool and start typing your mail merge letter. When you come to a place where you want to insert a field, proceed to step 5.
5. Choose *Mail Merge* from the Paste Special submenu in the Edit menu, or press ⌘-**M**. The Specify Field dialog box appears.
6. Select the field you want to insert.
7. Click the OK button. The field appears in your letter between double brackets << >>.
8. Repeat steps 5 through 7 until your mail merge is completed.

Give the layout a sensible name so you know it is a mail merge layout.

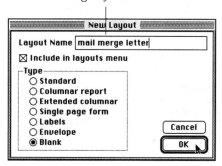

The mail merge contains fields that are surrounded by double brackets << >>. The text should probably be typed in the Body part.

Once you have selected the text tool, the cursor resembles an I-beam. Drag the cursor over the merge field, including the double-brackets << >>. Then you can delete or change the field.

We thought you might be interested in our special promotional sale this week. Your company, <<Company>>, has been chosen to represent the All-Kitty Pet Food Princess in |.

Make sure you select the text tool before you try to click in the text, or you will just get handles for the entire block of text and will not be able to edit the text.

■ Changing a mail merge

Mail merges are simple to edit. You treat the layout just like you were working in a word processor.

To delete a mail merge field

1. In the Layout mode, select the text tool from the tool palette.
2. Drag the pointer over the mail merge field, including the double brackets << >>.
3. Tap the Delete key. The mail merge field is now gone.

Changing a mail merge field

1. In the Layout mode, select the text tool from the tool palette.
2. Drag the pointer over the mail merge field, including the double brackets << >>.
3. Choose *Mail Merge* from the Paste Special submenu in the Edit menu, or press ⌘-**M**. The Specify Field dialog box appears.
4. Select the field you want to insert.
5. Click the OK button. The field appears in your letter between double brackets << >>.

Inserting a mail merge field

1. In the Layout mode, select the text tool from the tool palette.
2. Click in the text where you want the mail merge field to appear.
3. Choose *Mail Merge* from the Paste Special submenu in the Edit menu, or press ⌘-**M**. The Specify Field dialog box appears.
4. Select the field you want to insert.
5. Click the OK button. The field appears in your letter between double brackets << >>.

■ Layout suggestions

Labels are mail merge exercises. When you follow the steps in "Labels and envelopes" on page 31, the label layout looks like a mail merge with the fields enclosed in double brackets << >>.

Most mail merges are letters. Here are a few pointers to help you create good mail merge layouts for letters:

▲ You probably need only three parts for a mail merge letter (see "Adding parts" on page 35 for instructions on how to form parts in a layout). A common layout would include the Header, Body, and Footer parts.

▲ Use the Header part to place information you would use for a letterhead, such as company name, address, logo, or corporate art.

▲ Art can be placed in a Global field so that every time you use that field, that particular piece of art will show up. Global fields do not require data entry. The same item appears wherever that field is placed on the layout.

▲ Use the Body part for your letter.

▲ Use the Footer part to place special characters for the page number (see "Paste Special commands" on page 44 to understand how page numbers and dates work in FileMaker Pro 3).

✔ Tip: When you have created your text, complete with the mail merge fields, the text and fields become one item and can be picked up and moved around just like you move a picture.

This logo is contained in a Global field. Every time the Global field is used, the logo appears.

Use the Date Symbol command in the Paste Special menu to keep the date updated.

This footer contains the footer text and the page number inserted with another command in the Paste Special menu.

Printing & Help

■ Printing

You can print the record that is on screen, a group of selected records, or all of the records in any database. You can even print the scripts you have created. The exact commands you choose vary a little depending on what type of printer you have.

You can print as many copies of your database as you wish. Type the number of copies in the Copies box.

The Print radio buttons are unique to FileMaker Pro 3. These buttons help you select what you want to print.

```
LaserWriter  "LaserWriter II NTH"              7.1.2    [ Print ]
Copies: 1          Pages: ● All ○ From:     To:        [ Cancel ]
Cover Page:    ● No ○ First Page  ○ Last Page
Paper Source: ● Paper Cassette  ○ Manual Feed
Print:         ● Black & White   ○ Color/Grayscale
Destination:   ● Printer         ○ PostScript® File
Number pages from:  1
Print: ● Records being browsed
       ○ Current record
       ○ Blank record, showing fields [ as formatted ]
       ○ Script: [ All scripts ]
       ○ Field definitions
```

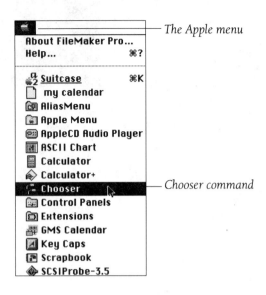

— *The Apple menu*

— *Chooser command*

■ Selecting a printer

While the Chooser is part of the Macintosh Operating System, not part of FileMaker Pro 3, you need to know how to use it to select a printer. You will find your Chooser under the Apple menu in the upper left-hand corner of the monitor.

To select a printer:

1. Choose *Chooser* from the Apple menu in the upper left-hand corner of the monitor. The Chooser dialog box appears.
2. Select the printer type in the left-hand panel of the Chooser dialog box.
3. Select the printer you wish to use from the right-hand panel of the Chooser dialog box.
4. If you need to activate AppleTalk, select the Active radio button. AppleTalk is used with networked printers, so if you're sharing a printer, you'll need to turn this option on.
5. Click the close box and return to FileMaker Pro 3.

If you change printers from the last time you printed from FileMaker Pro 3, check the Page Setup dialog box, as described in "Page Setup" on Page 180.

Close box

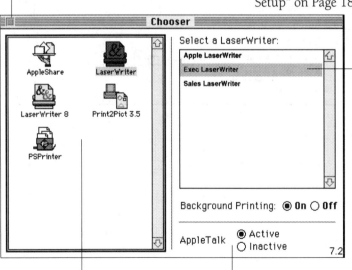

Select the actual name of your printer from this list.

Select your printer type from this panel.

Select the AppleTalk Active radio button if you are using a network printer.

Selecting a printer

■ Specifying what records to print

The Print radio buttons on the bottom of the Print dialog box give you several choices about what you print.

The records being browsed option prints the records you selected in the last find operation. To change the records that print, perform a new find operation specifying criteria that select the records you want to print.

If you select the Current record radio button, FileMaker Pro 3 prints just the current record, the record displayed on the screen.

Printing

1. Select your printer from the Chooser in the Apple menu following the steps given in "Selecting a printer" on page 176. If you change printers from the last time you printed from FileMaker Pro 3, check the Page Setup dialog box, as described in "Page Setup" on page 180.

2. Choose *Print* from the File menu. The Print dialog box appears.

3. From the bottom of the Print dialog box, select the Records being browsed radio button to print the found records or the Current record radio button to print just the current record.

    The Current record is the record you see on screen. The number of the current record is displayed just under the Rolodex.

    Blank record and Script give you additional choices. See the next pages on how to use these two radio buttons.

4. Click the Print button.

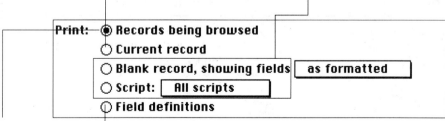

The Records being browsed radio button prints all found records in the database.

The Field definitions radio button is good for creating documentation or a record of how your database is constructed. Each field is listed and how the field is defined is shown.

Specifying what records to print

✔ **Idea:** *You could use blank records for instant fill-in-the-blanks forms to give to people, for example, in a doctor's office, or in any type of registration situation where people need to give you the information and don't have access to a computer.*

■ Printing blank records

You need two pieces of information to build a good record of how your database is constructed. You need to print field definitions (see page 179) and you need to print out a blank record for each layout. This shows you how you created your layouts and where things were positioned.

To print a blank record:

1. Choose *Print* from the File menu. The Print dialog box appears.
2. Click the Blank record, showing fields radio button in the Print panel.
3. Select the type of blank record you want to print from the pop-up menu.
4. Click the Print button.

For a full explanation of the choices on this pop-up menu, see the table below.

◉ **Blank record, showing fields**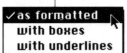

Printing blank record actions—Pop-up menu

Options	Explanation
As formatted	Prints each of the fields just as it appears on the screen, with no extra lines or boxes.
With boxes	Prints each of the fields on the screen surrounded by a field box. The field box shows the field's size.
Underlined	Prints each of the fields on the screen with the data entry area for the field underlined.

■ Printing scripts

Besides printing field definitions and blank records, printing out scripts is another level of documentation that is very useful. You can print the actions of each script and file them away for future reference, or loan them to a friend who might need to create a similar script.

To learn about creating scripts, see "Creating a script" on page 136.

To print a script:

1. Choose *Print* from the File menu. The Print dialog box appears.
2. Click the Script radio button in the Print panel.
3. Select the script you want to print from the pop-up menu.
4. Click the Print button.

◉ Script:	✓All scripts
	Sort and print
	change layout
	pause sample
	LAST INVOICE
	pause

Printing field definitions

1. Choose *Print* from the File menu. The Print dialog box appears.
2. Click the Field definitions radio button in the Print panel.
3. Click the Print button.

Printing scripts—Pop-up menu

Options	Explanation
All scripts	Prints every script in your database program.
Pop-up menu list	Prints only the script you select from the list.

■ Page Setup

Page Setup can change depending on the type of printer you are using. You should check the Page Setup dialog box whenever you change printers. Here is a common example and explanation of how to use Page Setup.

LaserWriter Page Setup

1. Choose *Page Setup* from the File menu. The Page Setup dialog box appears.
2. In the dialog box, select the type of paper you want to use from the Paper radio buttons or from the pop-up menu on the right.
3. Type the reduction or enlargement percentage in the Reduce or Enlarge box.
4. Select the proper paper Orientation, either tall or wide.
5. Select any of the printer effects from the Printer Effects checkboxes.
6. Click the OK button.

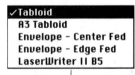

The Reduce or Enlarge box works just like the ones on the copying machine. If you enlarge your layout, be careful to have paper big enough to actually print it, though.

If you don't see the size of paper you want to use, select the paper from the pop-up menu.

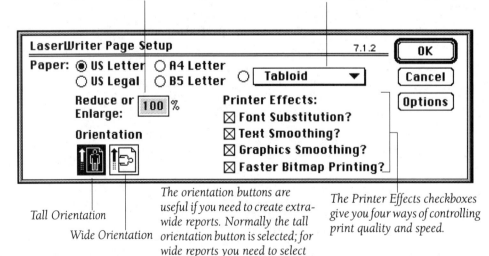

Tall Orientation

Wide Orientation

The orientation buttons are useful if you need to create extra-wide reports. Normally the tall orientation button is selected; for wide reports you need to select the wide orientation button.

The Printer Effects checkboxes give you four ways of controlling print quality and speed.

LaserWriter Options

If you click the Options button in the Page Setup dialog box for the LaserWriter, you find a whole new dialog box of choices.

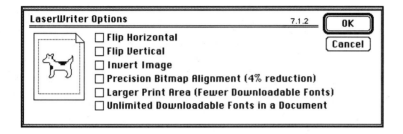

These checkboxes include options to:

▲ Flip Horizontal/Flip Vertical—flips the page either horizontally or vertically.

▲ Invert Image—inverts an image from white to black or from black to white, rather like a photographic negative.

▲ Precision Bitmap Alignment—reduces the image size by 4%, but makes the image sharper and more accurate.

▲ Larger Print Area—uses more printer memory to print a larger area, and therefore reduces the number of fonts you can print on a page.

▲ Unlimited Downloadable Fonts in a Document—keeps downloading fonts as you need them, regardless of the number you use. Be careful of this choice, though; your print area will be smaller and some printers can't tolerate this much activity.

Page Setup

Once you tell the printer to print, the PrintMonitor will appear on the Application menu. Click on the PrintMonitor icon to see the PrintMonitor dialog box.

■ Stopping printing

Sometimes you can't cancel your printing request from FileMaker Pro 3 and you must use Print-Monitor from the Application menu:

1. Choose *PrintMonitor* from the Application menu. The PrintMonitor dialog box appears.

2. Click the Cancel Printing button to immediately stop printing.

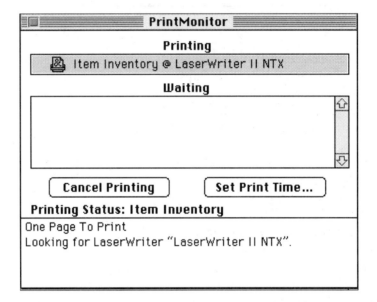

This is the PrintMonitor dialog box. Click on the Cancel Printing button to stop your job from printing. To see why your work might not be printing:

▲ *Check to see if the printer is plugged in.*

▲ *Check to see if the printer is turned on.*

▲ *Check to see if the printer online light is lit.*

▲ *Check to see if the printer has paper.*

If all of that is true, turn the printer off for 10 seconds, then turn it back on. It's amazing how many problems that will fix!

■ Help!

Uh-oh! In a jam? Try FileMaker Pro 3's Help. It's complete and easy to use—almost like having an online consultant!

Starting Help

There are two ways to access Help in FileMaker Pro 3:

▲ Press ⌘-?

or

▲ Turn on Balloon Help and when your pointer passes over an icon, menu, or FileMaker Pro 3 button, a little balloon will tell you what each feature does.

Using Help

1. Start Help by pressing ⌘-?. The Help dialog box appears.
2. Type a word or phrase that describes what you need help about in the Help dialog box. As you type, the topic you want will appear on the screen.

The Help Index is like a table of contents, listing all of the items contained in the online Help.

✔ **Tip:** *You can print any Help topic while you are in Help and you can see your topic on the screen by choosing Print from the File menu; or if you are really brave, have a large paper supply, and a lot of time on your hands, you can choose Print All Topics from the File menu.*

Here is where you type what you need help about.

Help is very automatic. You will see your Help screen appear below the box where you typed your Help word or phrase.

History keeps track of where you have been in Help while you are working in FileMaker Pro 3. History keeps recording your accesses to Help until you stop using FileMaker Pro 3 for that session.

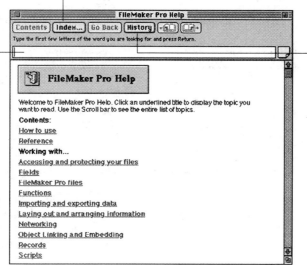

More help

Help is on its way in this example. As the phrase "access privileges" is typed, the words you type appear in black—FileMaker Pro 3 guesses what you are looking for and fills in the rest in light gray. The dialog box begins to display help for that topic immediately.

Here is where the Help phrase is being typed.

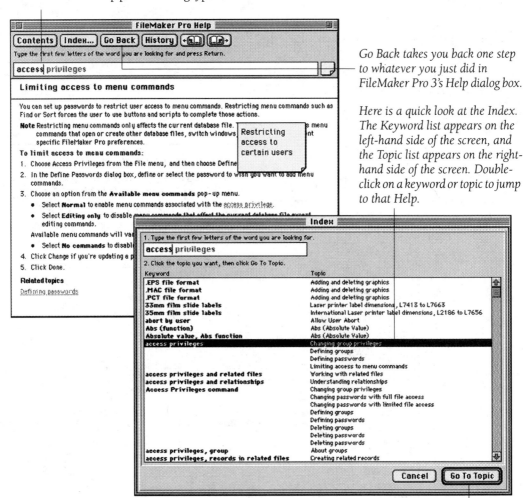

Go Back takes you back one step to whatever you just did in FileMaker Pro 3's Help dialog box.

Here is a quick look at the Index. The Keyword list appears on the left-hand side of the screen, and the Topic list appears on the right-hand side of the screen. Double-click on a keyword or topic to jump to that Help.

You can also move to a topic by selecting the topic, then clicking the Go To Topic button in the Index dialog box.

■ Using the "jumps"

If you don't find exactly what you need in the dialog box using the Index, but you come close, watch out for underlined text. These are jumps. Click on an underlined phrase and you will jump to the appropriate Help screen.

Remember, if you get lost, the History button will help you find your way back.

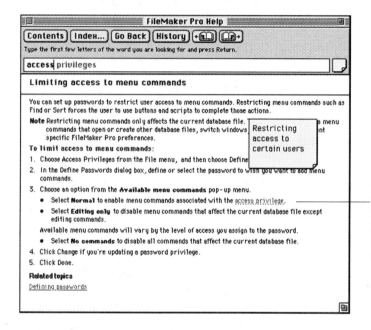

Here is a "jump" you could use to find out more about access privileges. Click on it and you'll move to a new Help screen.

■ Bookmarks

In case you need to find your place in Help again, you can add a bookmark to the spot you found.

Adding bookmarks

1. While looking at the topic you wish to mark, choose *Set Bookmarks* from the Bookmarks menu.
2. Type a new name in the Name box.
3. Choose a key from the Command key pop-up menu for quick access to this Help screen.
4. Click the OK button.

Deleting bookmarks

1. While displaying Help, choose *Edit Bookmarks* from the Bookmarks menu.
2. Select the name of the bookmark you want to delete from the bookmarks list. The Edit Bookmarks dialog box appears.
3. Click the Delete Bookmark button.
4. Click the OK button.

Changing bookmarks

1. While displaying Help, choose *Edit Bookmarks* from the Bookmarks menu.
2. Select the name of the bookmark you want to delete from the bookmarks list. The Edit Bookmarks dialog box appears.
3. Change the name or the Command key combination at the top of the Edit Bookmarks dialog box.
4. Click the OK button.

Using bookmarks

▲ In the Help menu, choose a bookmark name from the Bookmarks menu;
or
▲ Press the key combination for the bookmark.

The Bookmarks menu lets you create, delete, or change bookmarks.

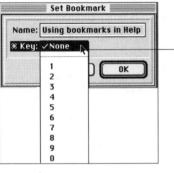

The Set Bookmark dialog box lets you choose between combinations of the Command key and a number to quickly access a particular Help topic.

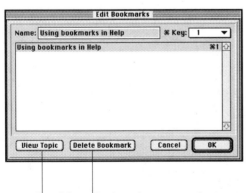

As well as deleting bookmarks, you can also view a bookmark from the Edit Bookmarks dialog box.

■ Attaching notes

If you're addicted to yellow sticky notes, you can add notes to your Help screens.

> This is really
> what a note looks like!

To attach a note in a Help screen:

1. In the Help menu, select the note icon at the top of the Help screen.

2. Drag the icon into the topic where you would like to make a note.

3. Type the text you want to have in the note. It's not obvious, but you'll have to press the Return key to end each line. Help notes don't line wrap like a word processing program.

The note icon

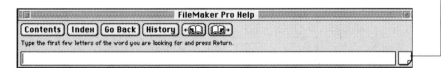

Deleting a note

1. In the Help screen containing the note, drag the note outside of the Help window.

2. When the note changes to a trash can, let go of the mouse button. The note will disappear.

Attaching notes

■ Moving around in Help

There are several ways of moving around in Help. Each method moves you in a slightly different manner and shows you a slightly different dialog box or menu.

This toolbar is found at the top of the Help screen. See the chart below to pick the method that moves around the way you like.

| Contents | Index... | Go Back | History | ◄▢ | ▢► |

Moving around

Type of move	Where you can find it	What it does
Jumps	Underlined phrases or words in text ted with the access privilege.	Jumps you to Help for that under-lined word or phrase.
Index	Index...	Takes you directly to the Index, which lists keywords and phrases.
Contents	Contents	Takes you directly to the Contents screen, which looks more like a traditional table of contents.
History	History	Takes you to a dialog box that tells you what you previously did in Help. You can then click on any item.
Go Back	Go Back	Takes you back exactly one step in your search process.
Forward/Backward	◄▢ ▢►	Pages you through Help topics, not by your previous moves, but by how they are organized in the Help manual itself.

Moving around in Help (side tab)

Modems & networks

■ Modems and FileMaker

Before you use FileMaker Pro 3 to send data over the modem, you must set the modem preferences.

To set the modem preferences:

1. Choose *Preferences* from the Edit menu. The Preferences dialog box appears.
2. Select Modem from the Preferences pop-up menu. The panel items change to modem items.
3. Type in the appropriate setup string for your modem in the Modem Commands panel's Setup box. This information can be found in your modem's documentation.
4. Type in the appropriate prefix. DT is the default prefix, and stands for Dial Tone. This choice is probably correct for your modem.
5. Type the appropriate hang up string in the Hang up box. The default choice is +++ATH. This choice is probably correct for your modem.
6. Select the type of connection from the Output pop-up menu. Choices include:
   ▲ Speaker
   ▲ Modem Port
   ▲ Printer Port
7. Select the modem speed from the Speed pop-up menu.
8. Click the Done button.

You will have to check your modem's documentation to fill out the Modem Preferences correctly. Make sure you select the proper setup string, prefix, hang up string, and dialing speed.

Modems and FileMaker

✔ **Tip:** *If you need to dial out of a Centrex system, such as an office or a hotel, in the Replace with box, enter 9,, (9 comma comma), then the telephone number. This dials nine then pauses to make the outside line connection before dialing the phone number.*

Select the location here.

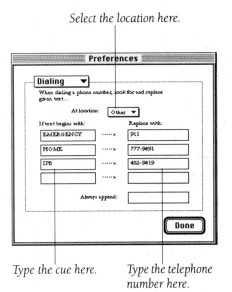

Type the cue here.   Type the telephone number here.

■ Using the modem

1. Choose *Preferences* from the Edit menu. The Preferences dialog box appears.
2. Select Dialing from the Preferences pop-up menu. The panel items change to dialing items.
3. Select the location for dialing from the At location pop-up menu. The choices include:
   ▲ Home
   ▲ Office
   ▲ Road
   ▲ Other
4. In the If text begins with box on the right-hand side, enter a value that is going to be used in a dialing field in the database.
5. In the right-hand box, enter the telephone number you want to have dialed when the value in the left-hand box is entered in the dialing field of the database.
6. In the Always append box, type any additional numbers you want the modem program to dial. For example, to append an extension number, your modem needs first to dial the number; pause while the connection is established, indicated by typing two commas; then dial the extension. The entire dialing entry should look like this: 763-2521,,8439
   Make sure you always want information in the Always append box to be added to every telephone number in the Replace with box.
7. Click the Done button.

■ Dialing scripts

You can dial from the database or dial from a script. To dial from a script:

1. Choose *Scriptmaker*^TM from the Script menu. The Define Scripts dialog box appears.

2. Type a name for the telephone script in the Script Name box.

This is what the Dial Phone command looks like in the Script Definition dialog box. Double-click this command to finish the script.

3. Click the Create button. The Script Definition dialog box appears.

4. Click the Clear All button to remove the preset script commands from the definition box.

5. Select Dial Phone from the Miscellaneous section of the Available Steps scrolling list. The Dial Phone dialog box appears.

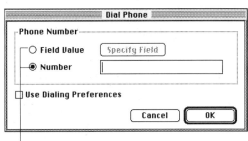

6. Use one of the choices explained in the table below to invoke the telephone number.

7. Click the OK button when you are done.

8. Click the OK button in the Script Definition dialog box.

Select Field Value or Number to invoke a unique telephone number.

Dialing options

Option/Explanation	Steps
Field Value radio button— When a certain value is typed in a field in the database, the telephone will be dialed.	1. Select the Field Value radio button. 2. Click the Specify Field button. The Specify Field dialog box appears. 3. Select the field you wish to use for the dialing from the Specify Field list. 4. Click the OK button.
Number radio button— Dials a specific telephone number.	1. Select the Number radio button. 2. Type the number you wish the script to dial in the Number box. 3. Click the OK button.
Use Dialing Preferences checkbox— Uses the telephone numbers in the Dialing Preferences (See "Using the modem" on page 190).	Select the Use Dialing Preferences checkbox.

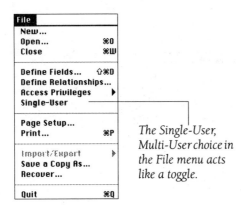

The Single-User, Multi-User choice in the File menu acts like a toggle.

■ Sharing networked files

You can share FileMaker Pro 3 files with Windows 95 and Macintosh computers over a network. There are a few rules that you must understand:

▲ The first person to open a FileMaker Pro 3 file becomes the host

▲ Other users who open the same file become the guests

▲ Changes made by either the host or the guests are recorded in the file

To host a file:

1. With the file you want to host open, choose *Single-User* from the File menu to make the file a multi-user file (the command will change to Multi-User).

2. Open all related files and perform step 1 for each related file.

To stop hosting a file:

▲ With the file you want to no longer host open, choose *Multi-User* from the File menu. The command changes to Single-User.

■ Closing shared files

1. On the computer that is hosting the file, choose *Close* from the File menu. The guests will see a Close File dialog box.
2. The guests must click OK within 30 seconds. FileMaker Pro 3 will wait for each guest to close the file.
3. If the guests do not close the file after 30 seconds, FileMaker Pro 3 will try to close the file.
4. If the guests continue to use the file after 30 seconds, the host will see a dialog box with a list of guests that are still connected. Click the Ask button to send another request to close the file to those guests.
5. Once all of the guests have closed the file, you can quit FileMaker Pro 3.

Troubleshooting networks

Problem	Solution
Can't see host database if you are a guest	Double-click the proper interface in the control panel.
Can't see a host database	Make sure you are using the same protocol as the host by checking the Preferences dialog box.
Need to remove a host from TCP/IP hosts dialog box	Edit the FileMaker Hosts file and remove the name.
Value list or relationship cannot be edited	Someone else is trying to edit the value list or relationship. Wait until the other user is done.
Unable to open FileMaker Pro 3 file over the network	Leave FileMaker Pro 3, then drag the FileMaker Temp folder to the trash and reopen FileMaker Pro 3.
Can't host a file	Make sure the network software is installed correctly.
Can't host a file because the menu item is dim	Make sure you are using the correct network protocol in the Preferences dialog box.

Appendix A
Functional formulas

Functional formulas fall into several categories, including: text functions, number functions, date and time functions, aggregate and summary functions, repeating functions, business and financial functions, trigonometric functions, logical functions, and status functions.

You must type the formulas in exactly the the same format given in the formulas and examples below.

■ Text functions

Name of formula	Function/Explanation	Formula format
Exact	Gives the answer true if two text or container fields match exactly	Exact(original text, comparison text)
Left	Counts a specific number of characters in a text phrase from the left and gives those characters as an answer	Left(text, number of characters from left)
LeftWords	Counts a specific number of words in a text phrase from the left and gives those words as an answer	LeftWords(text, number of words)
Length	Tells you how many characters are in the text of any specific field	Length(text)
Lower	Makes all uppercase characters lowercase	Lower(text)
Middle	Tells you the actual characters up to the middle of a text phrase	Middle(text, starting position, number of characters)

Text functions, continued

Name of formula	Function/Explanation	Formula format
MiddleWords	Counts a specific number of words in a text phrase from the middle and gives those words as an answer	MiddleWords(Text, number of words)
PatternCount	Looks through a text phrase for a number of instances of a pattern of text	PatternCount(Text, search string)
Position	Looks through the text for a certain numerically designated occurrence of a text phrase	Position(Text, search string start, occurrence)
Proper	Capitalizes the first letter of every word	Proper(text)
Replace	Replaces an old text phrase with a new text phrase you specify	Replace(old text, starting, number of characters to replace, new text)
Right	Searches right for a specific number of characters and gives you those characters as an answer	Right(text, number of characters)
RightWords	Counts a specific number of words in a text phrase from the right and gives those words as an answer	RightWords(Text, number of words)
Substitute	Searches and replaces text with new text	Substitute(text, search string, replacement text)
TextToDate	Changes an entry from a text date entry to normal date so math can be performed on it	TextToDate(text)
TextToNum	Counts a specific number of characters in a text phrase from the right and returns that as an answer	TextToNum(text)
Trim	Removes extra spaces	Trim(text)
Upper	Changes text to all uppercase	Upper(text)
WordCount	Counts the number of words in a text phrase	WordCount(text)

Text functions

■ Numeric functions

Name of formula	Function/Explanation	Formula format
Abs	Absolute value of a number	Abs(number)
Exp	Exponentiation; raises a number to a given power	Exp(number)
Int	Integer; gives the closest number to the number in parentheses but not any number greater than the number in parentheses	Int(number)
Mod	Modulo; calculates the decimal remainder portion of a division problem	Mod(number)
NumToText	Converts a number to text so that math cannot be performed on it	NumToText(number)
Random	Random numbers; generates random numbers	Random
Round	Rounds numbers off to a specified number of digits or decimal places	Round(number, precision)
Sign	Sign; returns the number 1 if an answer is positive and 0 if the answer is negative	Sign(number)
Sqrt	Square root; gives you the square root of a number or a number in a cell	Sqrt(number)
Truncate	Truncate; truncates or chops off a number to an integer or whole number	Truncate(number, precision)

Numeric functions

■ Date functions

Name of formula	Function/Explanation	Formula format
Date	Calendar date	Date(month, ,day, year)
DateToText	Changes the serial number of a date to text	DateToText(date)
Day	A number for the day of the month (example, 31)	Day(date)
DayName	Changes the date to a day of the week such as Monday	DayName(date)
DayOfWeek	Gives a numeric designation (1 to 7) for the day of the week (example, 7)	DayOfWeek(date)
DayOfYear	Gives a number for the day of the year (example, 321)	DayOfYear(date)
Month	Gives the numbers 1 through 12 for the month, such as 12 for December	Month(date)
MonthName	Gives the names for the months, such as December	MonthName(date)
Today	Gives current day's date	Today
WeekOfYear	Gives a number for a numeric designation of the week (1 to 52)	WeekOfYear(date)
WeekOfYearFiscal	Gives a number for the week starting with a given date	WeekOfYearFiscal(date, starting day of fiscal year)
Year	Gives a number for a year	Year(date)

■ Aggregate functions (statistics)

Name of formula	Function/Explanation	Formula format
Average	Finds the average of a series of numbers or entries in a field	Average(field)
Count	Counts the number of records or fields that are not blank	Count(field)
Max	Finds the maximum number in all entries in a field	Max(field)
Min	Finds the minimum number in all entries in a field	Min(field)
StDev	Calculates standard deviation of all entries in a field	StDev(field)
StDevP	Calculates standard deviation, weighted, of all entries in a field	StDevP(field)
Sum	Adds up a series of numbers or fields and acts as a container for a variety of basic algebraic formulas	Sum(cell beginning range..cell ending range)

■ Time functions

Name of formula	Function/Explanation	Formula format
Hour	Gives the number for the hour	Hour(time)
Minute	Gives the number for the minute	Minute(time)
Second	Gives the number for the number of seconds	Second(time)
Time	Changes time typed in 24 hour notation to a number	Time(hour,minute,second)
TimeToText	Changes time to text	TimeToText(time)

■ Summary functions

Name of formula	Function/Explanation	Formula format
GetSummary	Gets the summary statistics for a field as defined by a breakfield, which categorizes the summary statistics (as in sales statistics by employee, where employee is the breakfield)	GetSummary(summaryfield, breakfield)

■ Repeating functions

Name of formula	Function/Explanation	Formula format
Extend	Allows a nonrepeating field to be used with repeating fields when you create calculations	Extend(nonrepeating field)
GetRepetition	Shows the contents of a repeating field	GetRepetition(repeating field, number)
Last	Shows the last value typed in a repeating field before any blank fields	Last(repeating field)

■ Business and financial functions

Name of formula	Function/Explanation	Formula format
FV	Future value of an investment	FV(payment, interest rate, periods)
NPV	Net present value	NPV(payment, interest rate)
PMT	Payment	PMT(principal, interest, term)
PV	Present value	PV(payment, interest rate, periods)

Note: Each of the details of the formula, such as payment, should refer to a field in the database.

■ Trigonometric functions

Name of formula	Function/Explanation	Formula format
Atan	Arc tangent	Atan(number)
Cos	Cosine	Cos(number)
Degrees	Converts radians to degrees	Degrees(number of radians)
Ln	Natural logarithm base-e of a number	Ln(number)
Log	Common logarithm base 10 of given number	Log(number)
Pi	Gives the value of Pi, 3.14159	Pi
Radians	Converts degrees to radians	Radians(number of degrees)
Sin	Sine	Sin(number)
Tan	Tangent	Tan(number)

■ Logical functions

Name of formula	Explanation/Interpretation	Function
Case	Works like the IF function, but allows data entry, then decisions based on the data entry. (For example, if the number 1 is entered into the choice field, print; if the number 2 is entered into the choice field, go to the query screen, otherwise (default result) go to the data entry form.)	Case(test1, results 1(test 2, result2, default result))
Choose	Returns the first result (result0) if the result of a calculation equals zero; returns the second result (result1) if the result of a calculation equals 1, and so on.	Choose(test, result0(result 1, result2))
IF	Compares two conditions to see which is true. (For example: IF the field called State is blank, say "blank", otherwise say "unknown")	IF(Test, result 1, result 2)
IsEmpty	Checks to see if a field is blank	IsEmpty(field)
IsValid	Checks to see if the data entered in the field is valid as to form and content	IsValid(field)

Appendix A

■ Status functions

Name of formula	Explanation
Status(CurrentAppVersion)	Version of the application
Status(CurrentDate)	Today's date
Status(CurrentError)	Current error number
Status(CurrentFieldName)	Field name
Status(CurrentFileName)	File name
Status(CurrentFileSize)	File size in bytes
Status(CurrentFoundCount)	Count of how many records found
Status(CurrentHostName)	Name of host server on a network
Status(CurrentLanguage)	Language (English, Swedish, Swahili)
Status(CurrentLayoutCount)	How many layouts in file
Status(CurrentLayoutName)	Name of layout on screen
Status(CurrentLayoutNumber)	Number of layout on screen
Status(CurrentMode)	Current mode (Browse, Layout, Find, Preview)
Status(CurrentMultiUserStatus)	Current single-user, multi-user status on host or guest computer
Status(CurrentPageNumber)	Page number on screen
Status(CurrentPlaytform)	Current platform (Macintosh or Windows)
Status(CurrentPortalRow)	Current row in selected portal
Status(CurrentPrinterName)	Name of printer chosen in Chooser
Status(CurrentRecordCount)	Total number of records in database that are not empty
Status(CurrentRecordNumber)	Total number of records in database
Status(CurrentRepetitionNumber)	Current instance of a repeating field
Status(CurrentRequestCount)	Current number of find requests
Status(CurrentScreenDepth)	Screen depth in bits
Status(CurrentScreenHeight)	Screen height in pixels

202

Status functions, continued

Name of formula	Explanation
Status(CurrentScreenWidth)	Screen width in pixels
Status(CurrentScript Name)	Name of script that is currently playing
Status(CurrentSortStatus)	Status of sort: sorted or unsorted
Status(CurrentSystemVersion)	Operating system version
Status(CurrentTime)	Current time
Status(CurrentUserCount)	Number of users using FileMaker Pro on a network at one time
Status(CurrentUserName)	Name of current user

Status functions

Appendix B Installing FileMaker Pro 3

■ First steps

When you install FileMaker Pro 3, it will know whether you have previously installed FileMaker Pro 2 on your hard drive. For information about what to do with FileMaker Pro 2 files, see "Importing data" on page 161.

To start the installation procedure for FileMaker Pro 3:

1. Place the disk labeled Install in your disk drive.
2. Double-click the FileMaker Pro Installer disk icon on your desktop. The FileMaker Pro Installer dialog box appears.
3. Click the OK button, and the installation procedure will walk you through installing the files.

FileMaker Pro Installer

CLARIS®

FileMaker™ PRO ®
Installer 3.0

Remember to register your software to receive:
▶ Software updates
▶ Specially priced upgrades
▶ Claris Connections Newsletter

OK

You can let the Installer install FileMaker Pro 3 the way it knows best by leaving the pop-up menu set at Easy Install, or you can choose Custom Install, which will let you select various features of FileMaker Pro 3 to install.

■ Easy or Custom install?

Make it easy on yourself. Install FileMaker Pro 3 the easy way by clicking the Install button at the bottom of this dialog box.

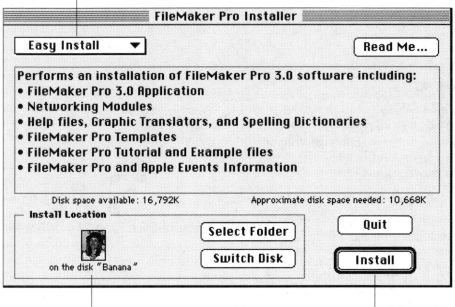

FileMaker Pro Installer

Easy Install ▼   **Read Me...**

Performs an installation of FileMaker Pro 3.0 software including:
• **FileMaker Pro 3.0 Application**
• **Networking Modules**
• **Help files, Graphic Translators, and Spelling Dictionaries**
• **FileMaker Pro Templates**
• **FileMaker Pro Tutorial and Example files**
• **FileMaker Pro and Apple Events Information**

Disk space available: 16,792K   Approximate disk space needed: 10,668K

Install Location

on the disk "Banana"   **Select Folder**   **Switch Disk**   **Quit**   **Install**

The Install Location panel lets you know which disk drive FileMaker Pro 3 is being installed on. This time the program is being installed on a hard disk called "Banana."

Click the Install button to get started.

During installation

FileMaker Pro 3 prompts you to change disks when necessary as it proceeds through the installation process. If you have a previous version of FileMaker installed, FileMaker Pro 3 may find that some files it wants to install already exist on your hard disk. A dialog box appears asking you if you want to replace the existing file with the new one supplied by the Installer.

"Home Inventory" already exists.

Do you wish to replace it with the file/folder from the installer?

Replace   **Stop**
Replace All   **Skip**

▲ If you created those files, click Replace or Replace All.
▲ If you aren't certain, click Stop.
▲ If you don't want to install these new files, but want to continue installing the program, click Skip.

■ Register your copy

Once installation is complete, you will see this screen, which signals the beginning of the registration process.

You can register
- ▲ By fax
- ▲ By modem
- ▲ By mail

Click the Next button.

■ Fill it in, print it out, fax it

Fill in the blanks with your contact information. Press the Tab key to move between fields (remember Chapter 4, "Working with fields"?).

Registration Information

Please provide following information about you and your copy of FileMaker Pro. To register your software, you must complete this information.

Name	
Business Title	
Company Name	
Address	
City State ZIP Code	
Country	USA
Daytime Phone	**Fax Number**
E-Mail Address	
Serial #	Please see your "Easy 60-Second" registration card.

Next

Then click the Next button to move to the next screen.

Purchase Information

Date of purchase:

How would you prefer to hear from us?

To help us serve your specific needs, which of these best describes the enviroment of which you'll be using your software?

Is this product ...

☐ Check the box to the left if you are be interested in receiving computer-related offers from companies other then Claris?

Previous **Next**

Don't give up yet! Fill in these blanks and click the Next button if you are happy with your answers. If you want to review what you answered in the previous screen, click the Previous button.

Fill it in, print it out, fax it

Finish it up and away you go

Fill in this last screen, click the Next button, then click the Print button to print out (or print to your fax modem). You're finished!

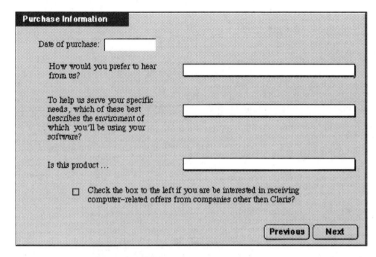

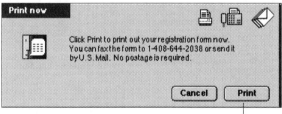

Last screen! Whether you print it, send it, or fax it, register your software.

Fill it in, print it out, fax it

Appendix C
Apple events

■ Script commands

Apple events send information and commands from FileMaker Pro 3 to other programs. You can use Apple events in a script to send information into an application such as Microsoft Excel or Word, then print the information from those programs, or create a chart within the program.

Creating an Apple event script

1. In the Layout mode, choose *ScriptMaker*^{TM} from the Script menu. The Define Scripts dialog box appears.
2. Type a name for the script in the Script Name box.
3. Click the Create button. The Script Definition dialog box appears.
4. Click the Clear All button to remove any current script actions from the action list.
5. Select Send Apple Event from the Available Steps scrolling list.
6. Double-click the Send Apple Event step in the Script Definition dialog box. The Specify Apple Event dialog box appears.
7. Select the radio buttons, options, and applications you wish to use for this Apple event. See the following page for details.
8. Click the OK button to close the Specify Apple Event dialog box.
9. Click the OK button in the Script Definition dialog box.

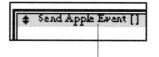

Click here to see the Specify Apple Event dialog box.

See the following page for a full explanation of the Specify Apple Event dialog box. Select the radio buttons and pop-up menu choices you wish to use.

Specify Apple Event

Target application: "<unknown>"

Send the [do script ▼] event with:

○ Document — [Specify File...]
○ Field value — [Specify Field...]
○ Script text

Options
☐ Bring target application to foreground
☒ Wait for event completion before continuing
☐ Copy event result to the clipboard

[Specify Application...] [Cancel] [OK]

■ Apple events details

The Specify Apple Event dialog box gives you many choices. The chart below will help you choose the one that is best for your project.

Specify Apple Event dialog box choices

Option	What you do
Target application	Application you want to open from the Specify Apple Event dialog box. **1.** Click the Specify Application button at the bottom of the Specify Apple Event dialog box. The file dialog box appears. **2.** Select your application from the file menu. **3.** Click the Open button. The application name appears by Target application at the top of the Specify Apple Event dialog box.
Send the [option] event with: Pick the option you wish to use.	This pop-up menu gives you four choices: ▲ Open application, which lets you open a new application. ▲ Open document, which lets you open a document to which the event is being sent. ▲ Do script, which lets you perform a script in the language of the target application. ▲ Other, which lets you manually enter an Apple event class and ID.
Field value	This pop-up menu leads you to the Specify Field dialog box. Select the field you want to use.
Script text	Type the script text into this dialog box.
Bring target application to foreground	Select this checkbox to open the target application in front of FileMaker Pro 3 so it is visible.
Wait for event completion before continuing	Select this checkbox to complete the Apple event before the script continues.
Copy event result to the Clipboard	Select this checkbox to copy any information, graphics, or data to the Clipboard for future use.

Appendix D FileMaker Pro 3 templates

■ Getting started with templates

Claris' FileMaker Pro 3 comes with three categories of templates: Business, Education, and Home. These files are set up and ready for you to use as models for your own information.

Here is how you use the templates:

1. From the File menu, select *New File*. The New Database dialog box appears.
2. Select the Create a new file using a template radio button in the New Database dialog box.
3. Select the category of template you wish to use from the templates pop-up menu.
   ▲ Business, which includes Messages and Names and Addresses templates
   ▲ Education, which includes Certificates and Student Records templates
   ▲ Home, which includes Home Inventory and Check Tracker templates
4. Double-click the template name in the template scrolling list. The File Name dialog box appears.
5. Type a new name for the file in the Create a copy named box.
6. Click the Save button when you are finished. The new template with the new name you gave it in step 5 appears on screen.

Select this radio button to use templates.

Templates pop-up menu

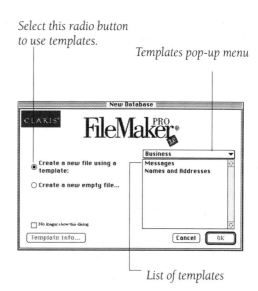

List of templates

Type a new name for your version of the template file here.

Business

Messages

Names and Addresses

■ Business

There are two major business templates you can tailor for your individual needs. You may need to change some of the buttons on each of the templates in all three categories.

Each template has two buttons on the end for you to define.

To change the buttons:

1. Create the template of your choice (Business, Education, or Home categories).
2. In the Layout mode, double-click the button labeled Your Own Button.
3. Select the action you want this button to take from the Specify Button scrolling list. For more information on creating buttons, see "What are buttons?" on page 143.
4. Click the OK button when you are finished.
5. Click the text tool in the toolbox and drag over the text label just underneath the button.
6. Enter your own label for the button and click outside of the area when you are finished.

The Messages template—Start using this template by clicking the New Record button. The date and time will automatically be filled in for you.

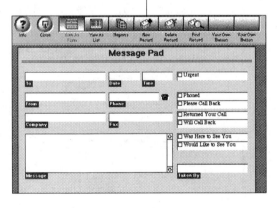

The Names and Addresses template—This template has a scrolling pop-up list for titles, such as Mr., Ms., or Dr., and a large scrolling field for notes.

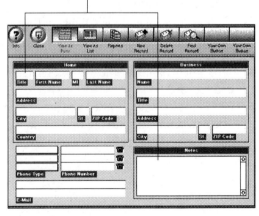

■ Education

There are a number of slick tricks buried in the FileMaker Pro templates. Here's another one—creating a divided layouts list.

To create a divided layouts list:

1. Create the template of your choice (Business, Education, or Home categories).

2. In the Layout menu, create a new layout by selecting New Layout from the Mode submenu, or press ⌘-**L**.

3. Choose Blank layout from the New Layout dialog box and click the OK button. For more information on how to create layouts, see "Layouts & parts" on page 27.

4. Choose Layout Setup from the Mode menu and type a hyphen (-) for the Layout Name.

5. Click the OK button when you are finished.

6. Choose Set Layout Order from the Mode menu. The Set Layout Order dialog box appears.

7. Drag the hyphen (-) to the proper position for dividing your list.

8. Click the OK button when you are finished.

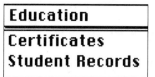

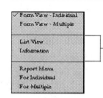

The line divisions make the menu more functional by dividing it into logical sections.

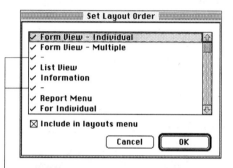

This is how the hyphen-named layouts look in the Set Layout Order dialog box. You can drag the hyphens to any position in the list.

Certificates template—You can design certificates for individuals or groups of people. The Type of Certificate field is a pop-up list that contains Certificate of Award, Certificate of Merit, and Certificate of Completion.

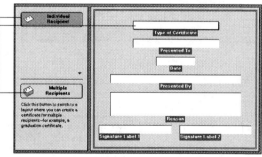

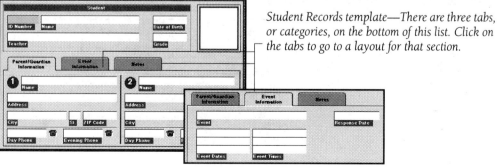

Student Records template—There are three tabs, or categories, on the bottom of this list. Click on the tabs to go to a layout for that section.

Home
Check Tracker
Home Inventory

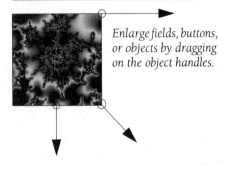

Enlarge fields, buttons, or objects by dragging on the object handles.

■ Home

The templates are good but they may not be perfect. You may need to enlarge fields.

A quick refresher on enlarging fields:

1. In the Layout view, drag the Body part down a little bit (or if the field that needs to be enlarged is in another part, drag that part down).

2. Click the field that needs to be enlarged.

3. Drag one of the handles to the left to make the field longer, or down to make the field deeper. See "Working with fields" on page 49 for more information on fields.

The Check Tracker contains a place to enter your checking information and a form that will print a check for you.

The Home Inventory template also has a place for you to place a picture of your inventory items in the form.

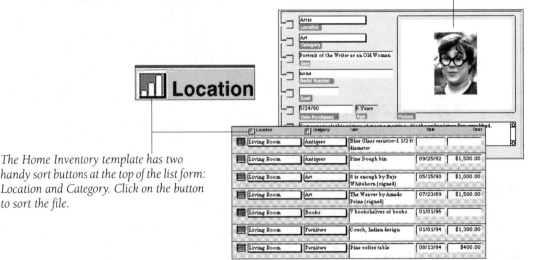

The Home Inventory template has two handy sort buttons at the top of the list form: Location and Category. Click on the button to sort the file.

Appendix E
Script commands

■ Control commands

Name of command	Explanation	Options
Perform Script	Plays a second script at the point in the current script at which you use this command, then returns control to the current script.	Script pop-up menu listing all of the scripts in the current database. Checkbox for any subscripts that need to be performed from the script list.
Pause/ Resume Script	Pauses or resumes the script depending on what is chosen in the options.	Pause/Resume options that: ▲ Pause a script indefinitely ▲ Pause until a field has a certain entry ▲ Pause for a certain period of time
Exit Script	Exits the current script.	None
Halt Script	Stops the current script from performing. while the user performs input.	None
If	This is the first part of a conditional script command that consists of: ▲ If (some condition that needs to be examined) ▲ Else (what will happen if the condition is not true) ▲ End if (ends the entire set of If conditional script commands)	The Specify options box immediately shows the Specify Calculation dialog box. An End if is present just following the If script command.
Else	*See* If	
End if	*See* If	Ends the If command that was starting by using If in the script.

Control commands, continued

Name of command	Explanation	Options
Loop	Placed just before a script command, Loop tells the script to repeat the action endlessly, looping and starting over on a continuous basis.	Appears with an End Loop command following it. Any actions placed in between the Loop and End Loop will continue indefinitely, until a certain condition is met, or x number of times.
Exit Loop If	Exits a script if a calculation results in anything but a zero.	None
End Loop	Ends a looping action when a certain condition is encountered, such as the last record is reached.	None
Allow User Abort	Placed on the first line of a script, this command allows the user to stop the script from executing using ⌘-. (period).	Presents two radio buttons: On or Off.
Set Error Capture	Moves any error messages from the screen to the Status(Current Error) function, enabling script debugging.	Presents two radio buttons: On or Off.

Control commands

■ Navigation commands

Name of command	Explanation	Options
Go to Layout	Moves you to any layout in the current database.	Presents a pop-up list of all of the current database layouts and a checkbox that will make sure the screen is refreshed.
Go to Record/ Request/Page	Moves you to any record, request, or page.	Presents a pop-up list that includes: ▲ First (record) ▲ Last (record) ▲ Previous (record) ▲ Next (record) ▲ By Number (record number) ▲ By Field Value (field name)
Go to Related Record	Moves you to any record in a related database.	Presents a pop-up list of related database files and a checkbox that specifies "Show only related records."
Go to Portal Row	Moves you to a specific portal row.	Presents a pop-up list that includes: ▲ First (row of portal) ▲ Last ▲ Previous ▲ Next ▲ By Number ▲ By Field Value
Go to Field	Moves you to a specific field in the current database.	Presents the Specify Field dialog box and a checkbox that selects the field.
Go to Next Field	Moves you to the next field after the current field.	None
Go to Previous Field	Moves you to the previous field before the current field.	None
Enter Browse Mode	Changes to the Browse mode on the Mode menu.	Checkbox option to pause the script at that point.
Enter Find Mode	Changes to the Find mode on the Mode menu.	Two checkbox options: ▲ Restore Find requests ▲ Pause
Enter Preview Mode	Changes to the Preview mode on the Mode menu.	Checkbox option to pause the script at that point.

■ Sort/Find/Print commands

Name of command	Explanation	Options
Sort	Sorts the database according to the most recent sort selections.	Presents two checkboxes: ▲ Restore sort order ▲ Perform without dialog
Unsort	Undoes the most recent sort.	None
Find All	Finds all of the records in the database.	None
Find Omitted	Finds only the records that were hidden when a Find was performed.	None
Omit	Omits or erases the current record.	None
Omit Multiple	Omits or erases more than one record.	Presents a pop-up list that leads you to the Omit Multiple dialog box and a checkbox that causes the omit action to be performed without a dialog box appearing.
Perform Find	Starts the Find operation up once a Find has been specified on screen.	Presents a checkbox that will restore the Find requests.
Modify Last Find	Allows you to change what has been typed in the Find screen.	None
Page Setup	Opens the Page Setup dialog box.	Presents two checkboxes: ▲ Restore setup options ▲ Perform without dialog
Print	Opens the Print dialog box.	Presents a checkbox that will perform the Print action without a dialog box appearing.

Sort/Find/Print commands

■Editing commands

Name of command	Explanation	Options
Undo	Undoes the most recent change made.	None
Cut	Cuts selected material.	Presents a pop-up menu that takes you to the Specify Field dialog box and a checkbox that allows you to select the entire contents of the field.
Copy	Copies selected material.	Same as Cut
Paste	Pastes copied material.	Presents a pop-up menu that takes you to the Specify Field dialog box. Presents three checkboxes: ▲ Select entire contents ▲ Paste without style ▲ Link if available
Clear	Deletes all information in a field.	Presents a pop-up menu that takes you to the Specify Field dialog box and a checkbox that allows you to select the entire contents of the field.
Select All	Selects all items in a layout when in the Layout mode.	None

■Field commands

Name of command	Explanation	Options
Set Field	Replaces the contents of a field with the results of a calculation.	Presents two pop-up lists ▲ Specify Field, which presents the Specify Field dialog box ▲ Specify, which lets you enter a formula in a Specify Calculation dialog box
Paste Literal	Pastes specific text into a field.	Presents two pop-up lists ▲ Specify Field ▲ Specify, which presents the literal dialog box where you type in text to be pasted Gives a checkbox option for selecting the entire contents of a field.
Paste Result	Pastes a calculated result into a field.	Much like the Paste Literal command, the Paste Result command gives the same pop-up lists and checkbox, but the Specify pop-up list shows the Specify Calculation dialog box.
Paste from Index	Pastes a field content into a new record.	Presents a radio button that leads you to the Specify Field dialog box.
Paste from Last Record	Pastes information from the previous record into the selected field.	For all four commands, Paste from Last Record, Paste Current Date, Paste Current Time, and Paste Current User Name:
Paste Current Date	Pastes the current day's date into a field.	▲ Presents a pop-up list that leads you to the Specify Field dialog box
Paste Current Time	Pastes the current time into a field.	▲ Gives a checkbox option for selecting the entire contents of a field
Paste Current User Name	Pastes the current user name into a field.	

Field commands

■ Record commands

Name of command	Explanation	Options
New Record/Request	Gives you a new record.	None
Duplicate Record/Request	Copies the entire previous record.	None
Revert Record/Request	Change current record back to what it was before any changes were made.	Checkbox allowing the action to be performed without any dialog boxes showing.
Exit Record/Request	Exits a record, or acts like clicking outside of any record to deselect all fields.	None
Copy Record	Copy the contents of the entire record.	None
Copy All Records	Copy the contents of all records.	None
Delete All Records	Delete all currently showing records.	Checkbox allowing the action to be performed without any dialog boxes showing.
Replace	Replaces contents of current record with choices from the Options panel.	Checkbox allowing the action to be performed without any dialog boxes showing and two pop-up menus: ▲ Specify Field, which takes you to the Specify Field dialog box ▲ Specify, which takes you to a dialog box that allows changes in current contents, serial numbers, or calculated results
Relookup	Copies or reenters information from a lookup source into current records.	Checkbox allowing the action to be performed without any dialog boxes showing and a pop-up menu, which takes you to the Specify Field dialog box.

Record commands

■ Import/Export commands

Name of command	Explanation	Options
Import Picture	Imports pictures into container fields.	Opens a dialog box where you select a file to import.
Import Movie	Imports movies into container fields.	Opens a dialog box where you select a file to import.
Import Records	Imports records from another database or file.	Presents two checkboxes, one that restores the import order, one that performs the import action without any dialog boxes showing. Also presents a pop-up menu that opens a dialog box where you select a file to import.
Export Records	Exports records to a database file.	Presents two checkboxes, one that restores the import order, one that performs the import action without any dialog boxes showing. Also presents a pop-up menu that opens a dialog box where you select a file to import.

■ Window commands

Name of command	Explanation	Options
Freeze Window	Stops any actions taking place in the window from showing.	None
Refresh Window	Redraws the screen.	Bring to front checkbox.
Scroll Window	Moves the window to one of five positions.	Presents a Specify pop-up list that moves the window to one of the following choices: ▲ Home ▲ End ▲ Page Up ▲ Page Down ▲ To Selection
Toggle Window	Toggles the view of the window into one of four conditions.	Presents a Specify pop-up list that toggles the window using one of the four choices: ▲ Zoom ▲ Unzoom ▲ Maximize ▲ Hide
Toggle Status Area	Changes the view of the status area.	Presents a Specify pop-up list that toggles the status area using one of three choices: ▲ Show ▲ Hide ▲ Toggle One checkbox to lock the status area view.
Toggle Text Ruler	Changes the view of the text ruler.	Presents a Specify pop-up list that toggles the view of the text ruler using one of three choices: ▲ Show ▲ Hide ▲ Toggle One checkbox to refresh the text ruler.
Set Zoom Level	Allows the zoom level to change by percent.	Presents a Specify pop-up list with zoom percents, and a checkbox to lock the zoom.
View As	Toggles between Form and List views.	Presents a Specify pop-up list with three choices: ▲ View as Form ▲ View as List ▲ Toggle

Window commands

225

■ File commands

Name of command	Explanation	Options
New	Starts a new database file from the File menu.	None
Open	Opens an existing database file.	Presents the Specify File dialog box.
Close	Closes an existing database file.	Presents the Specify File dialog box.
Change Password	Changes the password from the File menu.	None
Set Multi-User	Allows more than one user to use the same database file simultaneously.	Presents two radio buttons to either turn this option on or off.
Save a Copy as	Saves a copy of the current database.	Presents the Specify File dialog box.
Recover	Recovers a damaged database file.	Presents the Specify File dialog box and a checkbox that performs the action without any dialog boxes showing.

■ Spelling commands

Name of command	Explanation	Options
Check Selection	Checks the spelling of a selected word or phrase.	Presents a checkbox that will select the entire contents of a field. Presents the Specify File dialog box.
Check Record	Checks the spelling of the current record.	None
Check Found Set	Checks the spelling of any records that were found with the Find command.	None

■ Miscellaneous commands

Name of command	Explanation	Options
Show Message	Shows a dialog box on the screen that contains a user-specified message.	Presents a Specify dialog box into which a message can be typed or button captions can be changed.
Beep	Creates a beeping sound.	None
Speak	Creates a spoken message.	Requires System 7 and the PlainTalk Text-to-Speech extension. Shows a Specify Text to Speak dialog box into which the message is typed and a voice chosen.
Dial Phone	Dials a modem or telephone.	Presents the Dial Phone dialog box into which a telephone number must be typed.
Open Help	Opens the Help screen.	None
Open Define Fields	Opens the Define Fields dialog box from the File menu.	None
Open Define Relationships	Opens the Define Relationships dialog box from the File menu.	None
Open ScriptMaker™	Opens the ScriptMaker™ from the Script menu.	None
Send Apple Event	Starts an Apple event.	Presents a Specify Apple Event dialog box from which the specific Apple event is chosen, such as: ▲ Do script ▲ Open application ▲ Open document
Perform Apple Script	Performs an Apple script.	Presents a Specify AppleScript dialog box into which the script text is typed.
Comment	Inserts a programmer's comment into the script.	Presents a Comment dialog box into which the comment text is typed.
Flush Cache to Disk	Flushes any records held in memory to the disk.	None
Quit Application	Quits FileMaker Pro 3.	None

Index

U

V

W

Y

More from Peachpit Press

The Macintosh Bible Guide to ClarisWorks 4

Charles Rubin

This is a clear, no-nonsense book that shows how to get the most out of this new power-packed, yet accessible, version of ClarisWorks. It explains new features such as Styles for applying formats automatically to text; Libraries, a collection of clip art libraries containing 75 images; and ClarisWorks Assistants for help in solving personal finance problems. The book is full of tips for working smarter and troubleshooting sections for getting out of jams, plus a large section on advanced techniques. *$24.95 (520 pages)*

The Macintosh Bible Guide to FileMaker Pro 3

Charles Rubin

Completely revised and expanded, this new edition of Charles Rubin's popular guide covers all of FileMaker Pro's new relational capabilities, which are as powerful as other relational data-bases but easier to use. This volume's down-to-earth style and real world approach shows you how using the most popular database program on the market can improve your projects and your productivity. *$24.95 (500 pages)*

The Macintosh Font Book, 3rd Edition

Erfert Fenton

The newly revised edition of this lively typography primer demystifies fonts for beginning through intermediate Macintosh users. It provides clear, simple-to-follow instruction in basic typography concepts. Plus it gives the low-down on new font technologies, new ways to buy type, TrueType, and expanded coverage of legal issues. Containing 50 percent new information, *The Macintosh Font Book* reflects new procedures in System 7.5 without neglecting those of earlier versions. *$24.95 (400 pages)*

Visual QuickStart Guides

The *Visual QuickStart Guides* offer easy-to-follow, step-by-step instructions on getting the most out of these popular software applications. Hundreds of illustrations and succinct, jargon-free explanations quickly show you how to get around, without bogging you down with details on obscure, seldom-used features. Whether you're brand new to these programs or up-grading to the latest versions, the *Visual QuickStart Guides* cut out the fluff and tell you what you *really* need to know to get up and running right away.

☞ **ClarisWorks 4 for Macintosh: Visual QuickStart Guide**
C. Ann Brown
$16.95 (248 pages)

☞ **Excel 5 for Macintosh: Visual QuickStart Guide**
Maria Langer
$16.95 (272 pages)

☞ **PageMaker 6 for Macintosh: Visual QuickStart Guide**
David Browne
$16.95 (300 pages)

25 Steps to Safe Computing

Don Sellers

With planning, many computer-related health problems can be avoided. 25 Steps to Safe Computing tells you how to reduce your risk with well-illustrated, easy-to-follow advice. It contains ergonomic tips on setting up work areas, as well as chapters on backache, headache, tendinitis, radiation, pregnancy, kids' concerns, and much more. *$5.95 (72 pages)*

Order Form

USA 800-283-9444 • 510-548-4393 • FAX 510-548-5991
CANADA 800-387-8028 • 416-447-1779 • FAX 800-456-0536 OR 416-443-0948

Qty	Title	Price	Total
	SUBTOTAL		
	ADD APPLICABLE SALES TAX*		
	SHIPPING		
	TOTAL		

Shipping is by UPS ground: $4 for first item, $1 each add'l.

*We are required to pay sales tax in all states with the exceptions of AK, DE, HI, MT, NH, NV, OK, OR, SC and WY. Please include appropriate sales tax if you live in any state not mentioned above.

Customer Information

NAME

COMPANY

STREET ADDRESS

CITY   STATE   ZIP

PHONE (   )   FAX (   )
[REQUIRED FOR CREDIT CARD ORDERS]

Payment Method

❏ CHECK ENCLOSED   ❏ VISA   ❏ MASTERCARD   ❏ AMEX

CREDIT CARD #   EXP. DATE

COMPANY PURCHASE ORDER #

Tell Us What You Think

PLEASE TELL US WHAT YOU THOUGHT OF THIS BOOK: TITLE:_____

WHAT OTHER BOOKS WOULD YOU LIKE US TO PUBLISH?

MAC   **PEACHPIT PRESS** • 2414 Sixth Street • Berkeley, CA 94710